Praise for *Eat Happy Cocktail Hour*

"One of the hardest things about eating better is feeling like you have to miss out on the fun. Anna Vocino solves that beautifully in *Eat Happy Cocktail Hour*. Her cocktails and party bites are creative, flavorful, and designed to make the best of real life. It's a book that shows healthy choices and great hospitality can absolutely go hand in hand."

—Arash Hashemi, *New York Times* bestselling author of *Shred Happens: So Easy, So Good*

"I've known Anna for years, and what she does better than almost anyone is make food and drinks that feel joyful and make you feel good. This book has a refreshing approach to mindful indulgence, and captures exactly how Anna cooks and entertains in real life—generous, celebratory, and always delicious.

—Minnie Driver

"No matter what you're sipping on for happy hour, don't settle for anything less than spectacular. If there's anyone who can make your cocktail hour a whole lot more happy, it's Anna Vocino. Your kitchen will smell a whole lot better with this book in your hands. Cheers!"

—Abel James, *New York Times* bestselling author of *The Wild Diet*, podcaster, and musician

"*Eat Happy Cocktail Hour* is a game-changer. Living in dietary ketosis, I always thought the traditional party fare was forever forbidden fruit. Not so anymore! In her revolutionary new book, Anna Vocino has adapted dozens of beloved recipes to the low-carb lifestyle. She has also masterfully removed sugar from the usual syrupy cocktails by infusing a delicious blend of fruit essences and spices. I can finally enjoy my Sunday football just like everyone else. Thank you, Anna!"

—Vinnie Tortorich, host of the *Fitness Confidential* podcast
and filmmaker of *Fat: A Documentary* and *Dirty Keto*

"I've spent decades chasing great cocktails and ignoring nutritional facts, which probably explains my dad-bod. Thankfully, Anna Vocino has figured out how to make drinks that deliver all the pleasure with way less of the regret. Cheers to smarter sipping."

—Dan Dunn, host of *What We're Drinking with Dan Dunn*
and author of *Nobody Likes a Quitter*

"Anna Vocino has struck again and I'm intoxicated with excitement. As someone who's had a front-row seat to her kitchen sorcery, I can confirm: These cocktails, mocktails, and appetizers made me the main event at my last party. Thank you AGAIN, Anna. More please!"

—Andrea Anders (*Ted Lasso*, *Bookies*, *In a Holidaze*)

"Cocktail hour should be about flavor, fun, and gathering with people you love—not worrying about what's in your glass or on your plate. In *Eat Happy Cocktail Hour*, Anna Vocino shows how to keep the party going with creative low-carb cocktails, smart mocktails, and crowd-pleasing bites that still feel indulgent. It's a fresh take on modern entertaining."

—Eddie Zamora, The Yum Yum Foodie and host of the *Kill the Bottle* podcast

"*Eat Happy Cocktail Hour* feels like the kind of cookbook you reach for when you want to gather people you love and still feel good the next morning. I'm always looking for ways to entertain that don't revolve around ultra-processed ingredients or leave me feeling depleted, and this book strikes that balance beautifully. The mocktails are sophisticated without being fussy, the appetizers are full of real flavor, and every recipe feels intentional and nourishing. It's proof that you can celebrate fully and still honor your health."

—Cynthia Thurlow, NP, perimenopause/menopause metabolic and gut health expert

"I have enjoyed cocktails with Anna countless times over the years . . . some might even say that our combined decibel level indicated that we'd had a few too many cocktails! But we've grown up a little since then, and nowadays, we like our cocktails with less sugar and more nutritional accompaniment. Anna to the rescue! Reading this book and making these recipes is like being at happy hour with Anna today—she's given up all of the processed, sugary junk but zero of the fun! And no risk of getting booted from the bar when you're in your own kitchen."

—Sarah Baker (*The Kominsky Method*, *Young Sheldon*)

"Ready to enjoy cocktail hour without the guilt or health setbacks? In *Eat Happy Cocktail Hour*, author and chef Anna Vocino shows you how to savor every moment while following a whole food, metabolically friendly diet. Drawing on years of experience making your favorite recipes healthier, Anna delivers crowd-pleasing appetizers, snacks, and drinks free from fried foods and ultra-processed ingredients. Now you can stay on track with your diet—even during the most challenging time to eat clean—and still be the hit of the party. With Anna's recipes, you'll actually get invited back. Delicious, satisfying, and perfectly party-worthy, *Eat Happy Cocktail Hour* lets you have your drink and eat it, too. There is no need to 'cheat' when the food tastes this great!"

—Brian Lenzkes, MD, host of the *Life's Best Medicine* and *Low Carb MD* podcasts

EAT HAPPY COCKTAIL HOUR

Also by Anna Vocino

Eat Happy

Eat Happy Too

Eat Happy Italian

EAT HAPPY COCKTAIL HOUR

Deliciously Gluten Free and Low Carb Sips, Dips, and Bites

Anna Vocino

BenBella Books, Inc.
Dallas, TX

BenBella

BenBella Books, Inc.
8080 N. Central Expressway
Suite 1700
Dallas, TX 75206
benbellabooks.com
Send feedback to feedback@benbellabooks.com
BenBella is a federally registered trademark.

Printed in China
10 9 8 7 6 5 4 3 2 1
Library of Congress Control Number: 2026000722
ISBN 9781637749562 (paper-over-board)
ISBN 9781637749579 (electronic)

Editing by Claire Schulz
Copyediting by Karen Wise
Proofreading by Ashley Casteel and Lisa Story
Indexing by Debra Bowman
Text design and composition by Endpaper Studio
Interior photography by Anna Vocino
Cover design by Sarah Avinger
Cover photography by Anna Vocino
Printed by Dream Colour Ltd.

To Loren and Lucy, my favorite reasons to party.

CONTENTS

INTRODUCTION

Civilization begins with distillation.

—WILLIAM FAULKNER

TO THROW A PARTY, you need three things: people, food, and beverages. The most important of the three is people.

I believe life is meant to be celebrated, and people are the most important part of life. Without the people you love (and the new friends you have yet to meet), why are we even on this big, spinning marble?

I can't help you with your people skills. But I can help you with the food and beverage part of socializing. It's why I wrote this book!

I've been teaching people how to cook, grocery shop, and read labels for well over a decade, and now I recognize that when you find my work, you are most likely in the place I was 25 years ago: searching for answers on how to get healthy without having to completely sacrifice one of the best joys in life—food.

My Story

These intro pages may be the first words you'll read when you open this book—but they're the last ones I wrote. When I create cookbooks, I'm very focused on writing the best low-carb recipes I can and then photographing them in a way that will highlight how delicious they are, sweeping you up into a frenzy of excitement so that you will bookmark the page and add the ingredients to your shopping list. If I'm lucky, you'll make the recipe, snap a pic, and tag me on social media.

I've found most of you come to my work either from listening to a podcast I'm on or doing a search on Amazon for low-carb, sugar-free, or gluten-free cookbooks. And maybe you need to know a little more about me first. Twenty or so years ago, I was right in your shoes. Looking for answers due to a diagnosis of celiac disease, for which the only prescription was and still is not eating the dreaded gluten.

Back then, we didn't have pages and pages of search results with gluten-free recipes already adapted to be yummy and easy to make. Servers and bartenders had no idea what I was talking about when I'd have to go through the uncomfortable exercise of navigating a menu to find something gluten-free. Even Whole Foods, the only place I knew at the time that sold stuff labeled as gluten-free, didn't carry gluten-free food that actually tasted good.

So I vowed to take matters into my own hands. I set out to make gluten-free options with the intent that the food would taste as good as their gluten-filled counterparts. I blogged about it over at the now defunct Blogspot. And it was great—for a time.

Life happened: I was on TV shows. Then I wasn't on TV shows, but I worked as a voice actor (and luckily still do). I slowly put on weight and pushed my A1C into the prediabetic range. When I started podcasting with Vinnie Tortorich in 2012, I thought I'd be a wonderful comedic relief to his prattling on about quitting sugars and grains. I honestly questioned why I had agreed to spend the equivalent of a part-time job every week putting out free content on the internet (in addition to the hours spent food blogging).

I had no idea the Great Unseen had an even greater plan for me.

Vinnie taught me about what he calls NSNG®, which stands for No Sugars No Grains. Initially, I scoffed at the idea of it. I mean, I had done Atkins in the nineties, and giving up sugar felt like an impossibility. Especially considering I already sacrificed so much by kicking gluten to the curb so many years earlier.

But the idea of going low carb sure was intriguing. So in 2013 I tried it . . . and never looked back.

I revamped my recipes to cut out all the processed sugars and grains, and started furiously writing new ones. Then I decided to put the recipes into a book, which meant I needed decent photographs, so I went down a rabbit hole and learned food photography.

BARN
BITCH

THE BOT

I spent four years writing and obsessing over my first cookbook, *Eat Happy*. I put it out, but I was petrified how it would be received. I mean, I thought I was good at writing recipes people would want to eat . . . but it doesn't matter what I think. It matters what the readers think.

The readers liked the book so much, I released *Eat Happy Too* three years later. I had to top my recipe count, and they all had to be bangers (and they are). I burned out on cookbook writing. After a few years, my book agent Amy Collins coaxed me out of retirement to write my third cookbook, one near and dear to my heart: *Eat Happy Italian*.

A WORD ABOUT WINE AND BEER

In 2020, I moved full-time to wine country. It is a whole vibe. That fantasy that you have when you visit wine country—"Wouldn't it be fabulous to get a house here and live in all this beauty?"—is real. I did it. And I love it.

I've gotten to know so many winemakers here in the Santa Ynez Valley, which has seven American Viticultural Areas (AVAs) in Santa Barbara County. I even sit on the board of the nonprofit Santa Barbara Women Winemakers and Culinarians; our goal is to get more women involved in wine and food, and to raise money for our hyperlocal beneficiaries. BUT . . .

I'm so sad to report, wine has residual sugar in it.

NOT FAIR. But it does.

Any winemaker worth their salt will make a wine with the lowest residual sugar possible—usually 3 to 4 grams per glass—but if you are trying to watch your carb intake, wine will contribute to carb creep, especially if you have more than one glass.

Despite writing a ton about wine and loving wine, you will not find any recipes using wine in my books, whether in cocktails or in food. I am not against wine, as I personally enjoy it from time to time, but I'm against mindlessly consuming too much sugar.

As for beer: Regular beer is often one of the very first things to go when you quit gluten and go low carb. I haven't had a beer in 25 years, and I don't miss it, so beer is outside of the scope of this book as well (yes, even gluten-free beers, which there are a lot of these days).

What is this madness? I didn't sign up for this (except I did). I'm supposed to be onstage telling jokes or behind the mic doing the funny voices. But I've come to learn I have another happy place: the kitchen.

Five years ago, I founded Eat Happy Kitchen, a premium food company with the mission to nourish people across America with our clean and delicious pantry and snack items. It started with my marinara, a recipe I've been making since I could turn on a stove. Now we sell five flavors of sauce, four spice blends, and three cheese bite snack flavors. All delish and all made without any sugars, grains, seed oils, fillers, or BS. We are currently in over 1,200 stores nationwide, and growing every single week. Everything we sell has simple, clean formulas and tastes delicious. My mission is to bring some sanity and trustworthiness back into the grocery space.

Running Eat Happy Kitchen has taken over my life in the best possible way. It is my intent to grow the brand into one that is nationally recognizable. I hope that you will walk into a store and see one of our products and feel excited to purchase it because you know that not only is it delicious (duh, flavor is #1), but the lady who makes it is making sure these products are the best quality that money can buy.

When I'm not writing cookbooks, running Eat Happy Kitchen, or filming cooking videos for the worldwide internet, I am likely entertaining or on my way to an event where I need to bring a dish. Our house is the house that people swing by quite often. I love impromptu cocktail parties (and planned parties, for that matter). And I always wonder: Why should the gluten and sugar eaters get to have all the party fun? We can party like the rest of them and not feel like crap in the morning! But more on those tips and tricks later. If you have people stopping by the house, you will want to have fun making beverages and food that people love to consume.

Are Low-Sugar/No-Sugar Cocktails Even Possible?

Some cocktails are easy-peasy to make without any sweetness: the martini, the vesper, and many of the "1-and-1" cocktails—such as the Oh Be Joyful scotch and soda (page 58). But the architecture of a cocktail incorporates bitter, acid, herbal, liquor, and some sort of sweet. To get that sweetness, behind every mixologist's bar is simple syrup (1 part sugar, 1 part water) and a

bevy of liqueurs. Liqueurs are always sugar, alcohol, and a flavor, sometimes fruit-based like crème de cassis, herb-based like Lillet Blanc or St-Germain, or a blend of fruit and herb like Aperol or Campari. And so oftentimes, ordering a cocktail is asking for a big ol' glass of sugar.

Whenever I go to a restaurant that has a lovely bar program, I always ask which drink on their menu is the least sweet. Then I ask for that drink but without any added simple syrup, or agave, or whatever sweetener they use.

Every now and then, I am pleasantly surprised to be served a true no-sugar-added cocktail. But most of the time, I get a drink that's too sweet for me. Since I never send food back, I give that drink to my husband, who has learned this is how I operate, and I order a tequila soda with two lime wedges or a vodka martini, shaken extra cold, slightly dirty, with two olives. Hubs rolls his eyes and gives me his perfunctory lecture: "Stop ordering cocktails at restaurants! You never like how sweet they are." And I say, "You're right, sweetie." And we move on to dinner.

I'm no stranger to trying to figure out how to have a delicious beverage without overdoing the sugar. If you're quitting sugar, one of the first things to go is sugary drinks. It's a no-brainer—why drink a liquid that immediately sends your blood sugar into the stratosphere? When you know better, you do better. You quit sugary drinks, and then you quit fake-sugary drinks.

But a part of you still misses a celebratory beverage sometimes, whether it has alcohol or not. I know I did, so I started learning about the art of the cocktail recipe years ago. And now I am here to teach you.

Since distilled liquor has zero carbs, we will make our drinks with those. We are not using liqueurs or simple syrup in this book. We are getting off the added sugar train.

We *will* rely a bit on fresh fruit for some of the drinks. If you feel that fruit has too much natural sugar for you, no problem. Focus on the 1-and-1 drinks, which you can make special with bitters and herbs (like the Peach Mint Gimlet, page 61), or you can focus on the martini recipes.

Party Bites Made Low Carb?!

If you own any of my other cookbooks, you know that I love to re-create low-carb versions of all kinds of favorite foods. This book of party food is no different. I hope that these savory dips and bites will get you excited to entertain, or at the very least inspire some fun ideas about what to bring to your next potluck, event, or fête.

There is no shortage of fantastic appetizer/starter recipes from my three prior books. I love appetizers so much I could live on only appetizers for weeks on end, as they're my favorite way to eat. A little of this, a taste of that, all served up in bite-size portions and shareable with those you love.

I learned most of my party-throwing etiquette from my beloved friend and mentor Nancy Carithers (the inventor of the Oh Be Joyful cocktail). Nancy's cardinal rule: If you serve anyone even a drop of alcohol, you must serve them food. I don't want anyone getting drunk and sloppy, and feeding people is the best step you can take to help prevent your guests from becoming overserved.

I divided up the food chapters into two categories: dips and bites. I hope these new recipes will excite, surprise, and delight you and your guests as much as I enjoyed creating them.

As with all my books, the focus is low carb—but I live a real life that incorporates the occasional sweet treat. It is my intention to be the voice of reason in the very noisy diet space. So I included a few sweet treat recipes at the end of this book because sometimes you want to serve a bite of something sweet at your party.

As always with my dessert recipes: I use real sugar, no sugar substitutes or artificial sweeteners, and I never use any grains. Despite using real sugar in my sweet treats, I always use the least amount of sugar needed to make the recipe work. Once you quit sugar, you'll find that regular dessert recipes have way too much sugar in them. My dessert recipes are intended to be a sweet treat, not an everyday indulgence.

Now, let's party!

LET'S PLAY MIXOLOGIST

A QUICK GUIDE TO SETTING UP YOUR BAR

PLAYING MIXOLOGIST is fun. There's a *Portlandia* sketch about how the mixologist played by Andy Samberg takes an eternity to make one drink. This is not far from the truth. It's time-consuming to make a bespoke cocktail. That's part of the joy of it. When you are playing mixologist, you are not rushing to slam shots or down a 1-and-1 to get drunk. In fact, I hope the drinks in this book do what cocktails are intended to do: help you wrap up the day with an adult beverage (and perhaps share a bite with friends!) before moving on to eating a delicious dinner. Perhaps your adult beverage will help you make an even more delicious dinner.

A word about batch-making cocktails: While it's very possible to double, triple, or even quadruple these recipes to prepare a batch of cocktails, the focus of this book is making one or two custom cocktails at a time. To expedite your prep, you will want to make sure you prep all of your garnishes and ingredients in advance. Have your bar ready to go for when guests arrive.

Basic Barware, Glassware, and Mixology Tools

I don't mean to encourage frivolous spending, but you can really go down a rabbit hole to purchase so many fun things for your bar. Pretty cocktail shakers, cool retro glasses, silly napkins with pithy phrases, and shiny bar tools make you feel like throwing a party and, for me, are a must for setting the mood for cocktail hour.

I am well into the second half of my life, so I've spent a lot of time trolling antique shops and estate sales for vintage barware. The other person who lives in the house with me has suggested maybe I cull down some of the glasses, shakers, or bar linens, but I think he'd be wise to keep those opinions to himself, don't you?

If you're just starting to set up your home mixology lab, here are some of the basics you'll want to have on hand.

BAR KIT

Cocktail shaker: I recommend at least one cocktail shaker, preferably a Boston shaker—the one where the smaller cup gets inverted and inserted into the larger cup to seal the shaker via a vacuum seal, and then you strain through a strainer (sometimes called a Hawthorne strainer), which you also need in your bar kit. You most likely already have a cobbler shaker lying around at home, as that's the more standard shaker that comes with a bar kit you might have picked up at some point in your life. The cobbler shaker has the strainer built into the top of it, so you have to make sure you don't lose the cap that covers the strainer or else you've rendered your cobbler shaker useless.

Strainer: Preferably the aforementioned Hawthorne strainer, but any will do.

Long bar mixing spoon: Or use a long teaspoon.

Muddler: In a pinch, you can use the handle of a wooden spoon, but a muddler comes in handy.

Peeler/zester: I have four of these. That's not me bragging; there are just all sorts of cool peelers and zesters to use for drink garnishes and cooking, so buy what you're inspired to buy!

Jigger: For measuring.

Toothpicks: For stacking garnishes—bonus if they're fancy.

Ice tongs/ice bucket

Cocktail pitcher: If you want a pitcher to bulk mix drinks for a party, then let me enable you to make that purchase.

Boom, you've got yourself a bar set. For folks who drink their liquor neat (see below for the terms!), but you want it slightly chilled, you might want

to get whiskey spheres/rocks that can be frozen and used in place of an ice cube so that the drink doesn't get watered down.

BARWARE

For barware, there are so many possibilities, and you definitely should get creative with how you serve your drinks. Side note: "Up" means a cocktail without ice, "on the rocks" means with ice, and "neat" means pouring that liquor right into the glass without any prep whatsoever—like a larger shot, but for sipping. Boom, now you know all the cool bartender terms so that you get exactly the drink you want.

The essentials are as follows:

Martini glass (conical shaped, holds liquor served "up")

Coupe (shallow, wide, with a broad rim, serves mixed drinks served "up")

Nick & Nora glass (the hybrid love child of a martini glass, coupe, and small wine glass to hold cocktails)

Hawthorne Strainer
Muddler
Toothpicks/ Skewers
Jigger
Peeler
Copper Strainer
Long Bar Mixing Spoon
Peeler

Rocks glass/Old Fashioned glass/Lowball (usually holds 4–6 ounces, for liquor served on the rocks or neat)
Collins glass/Highball/Tumbler (usually holds 6–8 ounces, for taller mixed drinks served on the rocks)

If you'd like to spring for copper mule cups, silver julep cups, little tulip shot glasses, hurricane glasses, cordial glasses, tumblers, and margarita glasses, don't let me stop you. I'm a woman who has an entire section of my kitchen with a wet bar devoted to cocktails and coffee. As I write this, I'm looking at six cocktail shakers, every glass, mug, and cup shape known to humankind, and an extensive set of mismatched bar tools that I keep sloppily stuffed into the most exquisite crystal cocktail pitcher.

Lastly, I vote to keep your liquor bottles that aren't in the freezer on a pretty tray, collect as many ice buckets as you can fit in your bar area, and don't forget beautiful cocktail napkins and bar rags. Yes, even bar rags can be chic and set the mood, my darlings. And the mood I like to set is always rustic fabulous.

Nick & Nora
Martini
Flute
Coupe

Old Fashioned
Double Old Fashioned
Collins/ Highball
Tumbler
Rocks

Cocktail (and Mocktail) Ingredients

If you're like me, and you love being able to host an impromptu cocktail hour at a moment's notice, you will want to keep at least some of these items on hand.

SPIRITS

To make cocktails, you want a bottle or two of your favorite distilled liquors. Recipes in this book rely on these standbys:

Bourbon	*Rye*
Gin	*Tequila*
Mezcal	*Vodka*
Rum	*Whiskey*

Many of the recipes call for infused versions of these. I don't buy premade infused spirits like vanilla vodka or peach bourbon. They're often filled with added sugar and artificial flavors (that won't be disclosed on the label). See page 36 for my easy-peasy blueprint to make your own delicious infused spirits at home.

Standard cocktail recipes call for 1½ to 2 ounces of liquor. A larger cocktail or a full-size martini can have as much as 3 ounces of liquor, so please sip responsibly.

FLAVORING ELEMENTS

Beyond infused spirits, other ingredients can help you bring delicious flavor to your cocktails without loading them with sugar. Here are some flavoring elements you can bring into your low-sugar/no-sugar bar arsenal:

Bitters: These are super concentrated liquid extracts of herbs, roots, fruits, and/or spices. They come in many different flavors and flavor blends. Angostura bitters are a classic for the Old Fashioned. Other recipes in this book call for orange, peach, and/or lavender bitters. Beyond these, buy what calls to you.

Vanilla extract: Not just for baking anymore. Vanilla extract brings great flavor to cocktails!

Hot sauce: You'll want no-sugar-added hot sauce such as Tabasco or Tapatío for my Meaty Mary (page 62). A dash or two of hot sauce can add a fun kick to your next sip.

Teas: Herbal and black teas are a great way to bring in more flavor without added sugar. You'll see chai tea and hibiscus tea in certain recipes in this book.

Fresh fruits, vegetables, and herbs: You can get creative with the fruits, vegetables, and herbs you often buy. I keep all kinds of citrus on hand, especially lemons and limes, as they're heavy hitters for cocktail recipes, and I use them to cook as well. Other fresh fruit (whatever is in season) is perfect in a cocktail—squeezed, pureed, muddled, or chopped. Recipes in this book call for different varieties of berries, peaches, and mangoes. On the savory side I like to bring in cucumbers for their fresh green flavor and fresh jalapeños for cocktails with a kick.

Fresh herbs—like basil, lavender, mint, rosemary, and thyme—always add a special element to cocktails. If you garden, snip a few sprigs for your drink. Or if you bought a bunch of fresh herbs to use in a dinner recipe and have some left over, you can experiment by using them up in your cocktail, and let me know what you came up with.

MIXERS

Many cocktails—and all mocktails—incorporate mixers. Here are the ones you'll see most in this book:

Soda water: Always keep some sort of soda water on hand, whether it's a flavored water or just plain that you make from a SodaStream. Soda water is a fantastic dilutor of drinks while adding the fizzy fun. It also makes it easy to adapt most of these recipes into mocktails, using soda water in place of the alcohol. (Except for martinis: Those are basically pure alcohol, and there's no way around it. You can water them down by shaking them extra cold, 15 to 20 seconds, then let the ice melt for a minute or so, then shake once more before straining into the glass.)

Coconut cream or coconut milk: Canned *unsweetened* coconut cream and coconut milk impart wonderful creaminess to cocktails. I always choose full-fat. Note that canned cream of coconut is a different product and usually contains sugar.

Freshly squeezed fruit juice: A few ounces of freshly squeezed citrus juice imparts far less sugar than soda or fruit-flavored syrups.

JARRED GARNISHES

You'll want to keep jarred garnishes on hand to whip up impressive cocktails when the mood strikes. Check the labels for no sugar added. Things you may want to stock include:

Cornichons/gherkins
Pearl onions
Pickled jalapeños
Banana pepper rings
Stuffed olives (any kind you can find!)

A WORD ABOUT MOCKTAILS

Remember when I said earlier that the number one ingredient in a party is people? This may be a cocktails book, but a party that leaves out friends who don't drink or who aren't drinking that night is no party at all!

With the exception of the martinis, any cocktail recipe in this book can be adapted as a mocktail. You'll want to replace the spirits in the recipe with a mixer that will complement the other flavors in the drink. If the recipe already calls for a mixer, you can simply increase the amount of it to replace the spirit. Or you can get creative by bringing in other mixers that will complement the mocktail's flavors; soda water is always a neutral, versatile option, but you can have fun with brewed, chilled teas, freshly squeezed juices, muddled berries and herbs, and more.

Note that most traditional bitters contain trace alcohol, which adds a negligible amount to a drink, but it might matter for someone who strictly abstains. Choose nonalcoholic bitters, in that case!

I do keep a jar of Luxardo maraschino cherries in my fridge for my traditional Old Fashioned drinkers, but I prefer fresh cherries when they're in season in mine since I limit the sugar in my drinks. And fresh just tastes best!

Finally, *salt*. For certain cocktails, I like to use a glass with a salted rim. Finely ground salt works the best to stick to the rim of a glass. Many companies these days sell flavored salts for just this purpose, and if you like them, go for it. As always, I give my repeated warning—make sure to read the label to verify the flavored salt has no sugar added. You can get creative with salt and mix in herbs or citrus zest, pulsed in a food processor, or use smoky sea salt or lava salts in the Meaty Mary (page 62) or to complement the Mango Lime Cooler (page 39), if you're so inspired.

Watermelon Mint Martini, page 80

SIPS

INFUSED SPIRITS

YIELD: SCANT 16 OUNCES

A small handful of flavoring elements (your choice of citrus peels, chopped fresh berries or other fruit, sliced jalapeños, fresh herb sprigs, whole spices, whole coffee beans)

16 ounces distilled liquor of your choice (bourbon, vodka, tequila, etc.)

STORE-BOUGHT INFUSED SPIRITS ARE FORTIfied with hidden sugars and flavorings that do not have to be disclosed on the labels. I'm not going to take the time to email companies to try to find out what's in their mass-produced infused alcohol flavors. Instead, I like to infuse my own plain distilled alcohol with a variety of fruit, peels, spices, peppers, herbs, or even coffee beans. Some examples that are used in this book include cherry-infused bourbon, blackberry-infused vodka, raspberry-infused gin, coffee bean–infused vodka, lime and tangerine peel–infused tequila, and—yes—even cherry tomato–infused vodka (Caprese Martini, anyone? See page 76).

It's so easy to flavor alcohol with infusions, you'll be shocked that you didn't think of it before. Feel free to experiment with different flavors. Caveat about infusing liquor with spicy peppers and coffee beans: You really only need a day or so with both of these items. For whatever reason, they infuse quickly and give intense flavor to the liquor they hang out in. Citrus peels, fruit, herbs, and spices like cloves and cinnamon seem to take a little more time, so I tend to leave those in for a couple of weeks. And if, for example, you make a jalapeño-infused vodka that's way too spicy, you can dilute it with plain vodka and still use it.

Add the flavoring elements of your choice to a 16-ounce mason jar. Pour liquor to the top of the jar (depending on how much flavoring elements you've

used, you may use more or less spirit) and seal with the lid. I put a piece of masking or gaffer tape on the jar and label it with the date and the contents.

Store in a cool, dark, dry place to infuse. Shake your infusion jar every few days to help the flavor develop. Suggested infusion times:

Citrus peels: 2–4 weeks
Herbs and spices: 2–4 weeks
Fresh fruit: 2 weeks
Jalapeños: 1–2 days
Coffee beans: 1–2 days

Strain out and discard the soaked infusion items.

Keep the infused liquor in the mason jar in the freezer to keep it ice cold and ready to use.

MANGO LIME COOLER

YIELD: 1 COCKTAIL

THIS COCKTAIL HAS A LAYERED LOOK THANKS to the mango puree at the bottom. When you float each additional ingredient into the glass, you will slightly mix the mango flavor in with the tequila and lime for just a hint of sweetness. If you want to be able to stir the drink to incorporate the mango puree more, just serve with a straw.

1 tablespoon pureed ripe mango

1½ ounces tequila blanco or mezcal

Juice of ½ lime

Ice cubes

4 ounces plain soda water, or enough to fill

Lime wedge, for garnish

Plop the mango puree into a collins glass, then add the tequila and lime juice. Fill the glass with ice cubes, then float (this means pour in) soda water until you fill the glass. Garnish with the lime wedge.

THE ORANGE DREAM

YIELD: 1 COCKTAIL

Ice cubes

2 ounces vodka

2 ounces fresh orange juice

1½ teaspoons fresh lemon juice

1 tablespoon canned full-fat unsweetened coconut cream

⅛ teaspoon no-sugar-added vanilla extract

Dash orange bitters

Orange peel twist, for garnish

I PRESENT TO YOU A CHILDHOOD FLAVOR memory—like a Dreamsicle minus the sugar, plus the grown-up spirits—that brings the vibe of latchkey, sunshine, and rebellion that we of Generation X perfected.

Fill a cocktail shaker with ice. Pour in the vodka, orange juice, lemon juice, coconut cream, vanilla, and bitters. Shake until frothy. Strain into a coupe. Garnish with the orange twist.

THE BCC

YIELD: 1 COCKTAIL

BLACKBERRY-INFUSED VODKA SOLVES ALL problems—especially when shaken with some citrus and dreamy coconut cream.

Fill a cocktail shaker with ice. Pour in the vodka, lemon juice, and coconut cream. Shake for 30–45 seconds, until ice cold and chunks of coconut cream are pulverized. Strain into a coupe or cocktail glass. Float soda water until you fill the glass to finish the drink. Garnish with a mint sprig and/or lemon slice.

- Ice cubes
- 2 ounces blackberry-infused vodka (see page 36)
- 1 tablespoon fresh lemon juice
- 1 tablespoon canned full-fat unsweetened coconut cream
- Plain soda water, to float
- Mint sprig and/or lemon slice, for garnish (optional)

BLOOD ORANGE MARGARITA

YIELD: 1 COCKTAIL

Salt for the rim of the glass (optional)

Ice cubes

2 ounces white tequila or mezcal

1½ ounces fresh blood orange juice

2 ounces lime-flavored or plain soda water

1 rosemary sprig, for garnish (optional)

Twist of blood orange peel, for garnish

REGULAR MARGARITAS USE PLENTY OF LIME, a splash of triple sec, and lots of agave syrup . . . or, let's face it, more likely corn syrup if you're using a mix. If you can find blood oranges at your local store (or even bottled unsweetened blood orange juice), you can make a fresh take on a margarita that uses only blood orange juice for the sweetener. You can also substitute the freshly squeezed juice of a regular orange if blood oranges are not available.

If you'd like a salted rim, wet the rim of a rocks glass or margarita glass with lime juice. Roll the rim of the glass in salt until the edges are coated. Fill the glass with ice and add the tequila, blood orange juice, and soda water. Gently stir until mixed. Garnish with the rosemary sprig, if you like. Squeeze the blood orange peel over the drink to release the oil, then add the peel to the top of drink.

CUCUMBER MARGARITA

YIELD: 1 COCKTAIL

THE SHORTCUT TO A DELISH, SUGAR-FREE margarita is to infuse tequila blanco with lime and tangerine peels. Use it in this cucumber margarita for a most refreshing end to a busy day—or the beginning of a very fun evening.

- 2 Persian cucumbers
- Salt for the rim of the glass (optional)
- 2 ounces lime and tangerine peel–infused tequila blanco (see page 36)
- 1 ounce fresh lime juice
- 1 ounce fresh orange juice
- Ice cubes
- 2–4 ounces plain or lime-flavored soda water, to float

Using a vegetable peeler, peel one of the Persian cucumbers lengthwise. Wrap the strips of cucumber on the inside of a rocks glass or margarita glass. Run a lime wedge around the edge of the glass, then roll the edge in salt, if desired.

Chop the second cucumber into chunks.

Put the cucumber chunks, tequila, lime juice, and orange juice in a cocktail shaker and muddle for 1–2 minutes. Add ice and shake. Strain into your cucumber-lined glass, then float soda water into the remaining portion of the glass.

EGGNOG

YIELD: 3–4 SERVINGS

8 ounces heavy cream

8 ounces whole milk

4 egg yolks

1 teaspoon ground cinnamon, plus more for garnish

1/8 teaspoon ground nutmeg

2 teaspoons no-sugar-added vanilla extract

2–4 ounces whiskey, bourbon, or dark rum

SMOOTH, DRINKABLE PUDDIN'—THAT'S WHAT eggnog is. You basically make a custard, let it cool in the fridge, and then drink it right up. Of course this version is made without any added sugar, and I don't add artificial sweeteners or sugar substitutes. If you need to add sweetness, then you do you, and add it to taste.

Dark rum will give this eggnog more sweetness, as rum is a distilled liquor made from sugar with a sweeter flavor profile (although it has zero carbs). I prefer bourbon or Irish whiskey. If you are ready to brunch with your eggnog, you can pour a couple of tablespoons of it into coffee. You're welcome.

In a small saucepan, heat the cream and milk over medium heat until frothy, whisking to make sure a film doesn't form on top and being careful not to let the mixture scald on the sides and bottom of the pan. Remove from the heat.

Meanwhile, whisk the egg yolks in a heatproof bowl until light yellow and fluffy. Very slowly whisk a little of the hot milk mixture into the egg yolks, adding more and more hot milk to temper the eggs (that means getting them to the same temperature as the milk without letting them scramble).

Pour the milk and egg mixture back into the pan. Add the cinnamon and nutmeg. Bring to a light boil over medium heat, being careful not to scald by stirring with a wooden spoon. Cook for 9–10 minutes, until the mixture has thickened. To test the thickness, when you lift the

wooden spoon up, the mixture should coat the spoon, and if you swipe your finger across it, it will leave a line.

Strain the mixture through a fine-mesh strainer into a glass bowl. Whisk in the vanilla and liquor. Cover with plastic wrap, smoothing the plastic over the surface of the eggnog to prevent it from forming a film. Refrigerate until chilled, or even overnight.

Whisk the eggnog. Pour into glasses (a coupe looks nice) and garnish with additional cinnamon and good cheer.

Spinach Dip Low-Carb Crust Christmas Tree, page 182, and Eggnog, page 48

THE SPARKLER

YIELD: 1 COCKTAIL

THIS RECIPE USES BREWED TEA FOR FLAVOR. I love the tartness and inherent sweetness of hibiscus tea to complement a summer cocktail. The cocktail is fantastic to make late in the summer during peak peach season. One peach will be pureed to use in the drink, and the other peach needs to be frozen for 2–4 hours, until it's firm enough to grate into a garnish.

- 1 hibiscus tea bag
- 2 peaches, one pitted and chopped and one frozen for 2–4 hours
- 1/4 cup raspberries
- Ice cubes
- 1 1/2 ounces raspberry-infused gin (see page 36)
- 1 tablespoon fresh lemon juice
- 1/4 teaspoon fresh thyme leaves
- 2 ounces plain soda water, to float
- 1 thyme sprig, for garnish

Pour about a cup of boiling water over a hibiscus tea bag and let it steep for 5–10 minutes. Remove the tea bag and let the tea cool, then stick it in the fridge until completely chilled.

Meanwhile, puree the chopped peach and raspberries in a small food processor or blender until very smooth. Strain through a fine-mesh strainer into a bowl, discarding the seeds and fibers.

Fill a cocktail shaker with ice. Pour in 2 ounces of the raspberry-peach puree, 2 ounces of the cooled hibiscus tea, the gin, and lemon juice, then shake until cold. Strain into a stemless champagne flute or a coupe and float the soda water on top until the glass is full.

Grate the frozen peach with a box grater. Garnish your cocktail with the thyme sprig and some of the grated frozen peach.

CHAI-SPICED WHISKEY

YIELD: 1 COCKTAIL

1 chai tea bag

Ice cubes for shaking, plus 1 large ice cube for serving

2 ounces whiskey

1 ounce canned full-fat unsweetened coconut cream

1 tablespoon fresh orange juice

1 teaspoon maple syrup (optional)

Edible flowers, for garnish (optional)

HOMEMADE CHAI PLUS WHISKEY MAKES FOR A spicy winter comfort beverage. You can find edible flowers in the produce department of fancy grocery stores, but they are a completely optional visual garnish.

Pour a cup of boiling water over a chai tea bag and let it steep for 3–5 minutes. Remove the tea bag and let the tea cool, then stick it in the fridge until fully chilled.

Fill a cocktail shaker with ice. Pour in 4 ounces of the chilled tea, the whiskey, coconut cream, orange juice, and maple syrup (if using). Shake until frothy and cold. Strain into a rocks glass with a large ice cube. Garnish with edible flowers, if you like being fancy.

GIN LAVENDER

YIELD: 1 COCKTAIL

IF YOU LIKE THE HERBAL, FLORAL SCENT OF lavender, this cocktail will transport you to a beautiful May day in Provence. Grab some lavender bitters when you're next at the liquor store (I like Greenbar brand; it's also easy to find online), and you can pick up a tiny bag of culinary-grade lavender from any bulk herb store.

- Ice cubes
- 1½ ounces raspberry-infused gin (see page 36)
- 1½ teaspoons fresh lime juice
- Dash lavender bitters
- Plain soda water, to float
- Pinch crushed lavender flowers, for garnish

Fill a cocktail shaker with ice. Pour in the gin, lime juice, and lavender bitters. Shake until ice cold, 15–20 seconds. Strain into a coupe or martini glass and float soda water until the glass is full. Garnish with the crushed lavender flowers.

OH BE JOYFUL

YIELD: 1 COCKTAIL

Ice cubes

1½ ounces scotch

2–4 ounces plain soda water

Lime wedge, for garnish

THE 1-AND-1 COCKTAILS ARE THE FRIENDLIEST to low-carbers trying to cut back on sugar but still have a grown-up beverage. A vodka soda, tequila and soda, whiskey and soda are all simple preparations, usually spruced up with a squeeze of fresh lime juice.

Since the 1-and-1 cocktail is well known and easy to make, you may not even need a recipe—but I am highlighting just one, made famous by Nancy Carithers, who happens to be the mother of Haven, one of my bestest and longtime friends and godmother to Lucy. If you read this book's introduction, you will know that Nancy is responsible for teaching me early on how to throw a good party, and so I'm honoring her here by sharing the recipe for Nancy's Oh Be Joyful, which Haven can make in her sleep.

And while an Oh Be Joyful is a drink, it's also a mood as you exclaim at 5 PM, "Who's ready for their Oh Be Joyful?" just like Nancy does.

Pour the scotch and soda water into an ice-packed rocks glass. Finish with a squeeze of lime juice, toss in the lime wedge, and stir, then toast to it being 5 PM.

PEACH MINT GIMLET

YIELD: 1 COCKTAIL

TAKING A 1-AND-1 TO THE NEXT LEVEL IS what the gimlet does so well. My two favorite taste sensations of the summer are peach and mint. Put them together into one cocktail, and you've got the perfect gimlet. Peach bitters are easy to find in any fancy liquor store or online, so you don't have to wait until peach season to make this refreshing cocktail.

In a cocktail shaker, muddle the vodka, lime juice, and a small handful of mint leaves for 1–2 minutes. Add ice to the shaker and shake for 20–30 seconds. Put 1–2 additional mint sprigs in a rocks glass, then fill the glass with ice. Strain the contents of the shaker into the glass. Float soda water on top until you fill the glass, then add a few drops of peach bitters.

2 ounces vodka or gin

1 ounce fresh lime juice

Mint sprigs, for muddling and garnish

Ice cubes

Plain or peach-flavored soda water, to float

Dash peach bitters

THE MEATY MARY

YIELD: 1 COCKTAIL

TO RIM THE GLASS (OPTIONAL)

Sea salt

1 tablespoon smoked paprika

Bacon grease, at room temperature, or olive oil

COCKTAIL

Ice cubes

2 ounces vodka

¾ cup (6 ounces) Eat Happy Kitchen Marinara Sauce, or use your favorite brand

1 tablespoon pickle brine

¼ teaspoon prepared horseradish

¼ teaspoon Worcestershire sauce

¼ teaspoon no-sugar-added hot sauce

¼ teaspoon celery salt

¼ teaspoon smoked paprika

Freshly ground black pepper

Plain soda water, to float (optional)

GARNISHES

Pimento-stuffed olives

Dill pickle spear

Celery stalk

1–2 crispy cooked bacon strips

3–4 Butter-Poached Shrimp (page 159)

THIS CLASSIC COCKTAIL IS BRUNCH IN A GLASS. You can get creative and add any sort of protein as a garnish—grilled meats, leftover chunks of pot roast, heck, even a soft-boiled egg would be perfect—but in the following recipe I suggest crispy bacon strips and my Butter-Poached Shrimp (page 159). We're all told we need to eat more protein, so who's to say we can't combine that with a spicy, tomatoey vodka drink in a highball?

I use Eat Happy Kitchen Marinara Sauce in place of plain tomato juice and Clamato for simplicity. If you're using another brand of marinara, be sure to check the label to make sure there's no added sugar. If you're making homemade bacon for this drink, you can reserve the bacon grease to help the salt and smoked paprika stick to the rim of the glass. Olive oil will also serve the same purpose.

If you'd like a seasoned rim, in a shallow dish, combine the sea salt and smoked paprika and stir together. Roll the rim of a highball glass in room-temperature bacon grease or olive oil, then roll in the salt-paprika mix.

Fill a cocktail shaker with ice. Pour in the vodka, marinara, pickle brine, horseradish, Worcestershire sauce, hot sauce, celery salt, smoked paprika, and a few twists of freshly ground black pepper. Shake until ice cold, about 30 seconds. Strain into a highball glass and float soda water to fill the glass if desired. Garnish with an extra twist of pepper, plus olives, a pickle, celery, crispy bacon strips, and shrimp.

FROZÉ

YIELD: 4–5 COCKTAILS

I'VE NEVER BEEN MUCH OF A DAY DRINKER, but when I do, this frozé hits the spot. It's a granita type of drink, typically made with cheap rosé wine and vodka. In this sugar-free version, hibiscus tea and strawberries mimic the flavor notes in rosé wine, and the natural sweetness of the strawberries brings it all together.

3 cups ice cubes

6 ounces vodka

8 ounces hibiscus tea, brewed and cooled in the fridge

1½ cups strawberries, tops cut off and discarded, plus more whole strawberries for garnish

In a high-speed blender, puree all the ingredients together for 10–15 seconds, until smooth and frothy, being careful not to overblend, as it will melt the ice. If you do overblend, you can add more ice. Pour into 4 or 5 cocktail glasses and serve, garnished with fresh strawberries.

MOCKTAIL VARIATION:

Omit the vodka and blend together the ice, hibiscus tea, and strawberries until smooth. Pour into glasses and float 2–3 ounces soda water into each cocktail.

KENTUCKY MULE

YIELD: 1 COCKTAIL

- 2 ounces whiskey of choice (rye, bourbon, or any favorite whiskey)
- 1 ounce fresh lime juice, plus 1 lime wedge for garnish
- ½ teaspoon grated fresh ginger
- Fresh mint, for muddling and for garnish
- Ice cubes
- 2 ounces lime-flavored soda water, to float

THE MOSCOW MULE IS A VERY POPULAR COCKtail for a reason: It's delish. But it is very sweet because of the ginger beer. I also love making mine with a brown liquor, and when you pair whiskey with fresh ginger and lime, the thought of ginger beer will become a distant memory. Tip: If you can find Polar Seltzer Ginger Lime Mule flavor, it is perfect for this—but if you can't, plain lime is just fine.

In a copper mug, muddle the whiskey, lime juice, ginger, and a small handful of mint leaves for 1 minute, until fragrant. Fill the mug with ice, then float the soda water until the glass is full. Garnish with a lime wedge and mint sprigs.

OLD FASHIONED

YIELD: 1 COCKTAIL

CHERRY-INFUSED BOURBON PROVIDES EXTRA perceived sweetness without the added sugar. To make your old fashioned last longer, you can float some orange-flavored soda water in it.

If you can find large ice cubes, they are perfect for serving an old fashioned, as the ice melts slowly to cool down your drink at the perfect pace while you imbibe.

- 2 ounces cherry-infused bourbon (see page 36)
- 2 dashes Angostura bitters or orange bitters
- Ice cubes for stirring, plus 1 large ice cube for serving
- 1 orange wedge
- Fresh cherries, halved and pitted, for garnish
- Orange peel, for garnish

Pour the bourbon and bitters over ice in a glass pitcher. Stir with a long spoon until the ice cools the bourbon, 1–2 minutes. Place a large ice cube in a rocks glass and squeeze the orange wedge into the glass. Pour the bourbon over the ice cube and garnish with a few fresh cherries. Twist the orange peel over the glass and rub the peel over the rim of the glass, then drop the peel into the glass.

BOOZY GINGER PEACH POPS

YIELD: 5–6 POPS, DEPENDING ON ICE POP MOLD SIZE

4–5 ripe peaches, pitted and sliced

2 teaspoons grated fresh ginger

Juice of 1 lemon

2½ ounces vodka

THIS ICE POP RECIPE IS SIMPLE IN ITS INGREdients, but the combination of flavors will remind you of a gourmet boozy pop. Make sure you use ripe peaches and measure your vodka carefully to be sure the pops will harden in the freezer. This also makes a great no-added-sugar ice pop for anyone to enjoy; just omit the vodka for a mocksicle.

Puree all the ingredients in a high-speed blender until smooth. Pour equal amounts into ice pop molds and freeze for at least 6 hours, until solid. Remove from the freezer 10 minutes before serving to soften the pops enough to remove them cleanly from the molds.

A WORD ON MARTINIS

Martinis are fun, elegant, and inviting. From the sound the shaker makes to the ability to personalize it to your heart's content, the martini is the ultimate bespoke cocktail.

A basic martini is a swirl of vermouth in a glass, then gin or vodka, shaken or stirred over ice, served cold and straight up, then garnished however the recipient prefers. From there, you can customize with any variety of flavor profiles you want, from briny to savory to sweet. It's the big daddy OG of cocktails, and I hope these recipes for creative martini variations whet your 5 PM whistle.

Villa Cappelli Olive Oil Martini, page 83

CAPRESE MARTINI

YIELD: 2 COCKTAILS

- 6–8 fresh basil leaves, loosely chopped, plus whole leaves for garnish
- 3 tablespoons flaky sea salt
- 1 tablespoon olive oil
- ½ teaspoon balsamic vinegar, divided
- Ice cubes
- 6 ounces cherry tomato–infused vodka (see page 36)
- Cherry tomatoes and small mozzarella balls, for garnish

IF YOUR GOAL IS TO GET YOUR GUESTS TO OOH and aah at your cocktail prowess, this is the showstopper drink to craft. They don't need to know it's easy to make. Serve at the beginning of an incredible Italian meal, and you will be elevated to god-tier status.

To prep the martini glass rims, in a mini food processor or small blender, pulse the basil leaves and sea salt until pulverized and fine, then pour the salt mix onto a small plate. On a second small plate, pour the olive oil, then coat the top of each martini glass with the olive oil. Roll the oiled glass edges into the basil salt mixture to rim the glass.

Pour ¼ teaspoon balsamic vinegar at the center of each martini glass bottom.

Fill a cocktail shaker with ice. Pour in the vodka and shake for 20–30 seconds, then strain into the rimmed glasses. Thread a few cherry tomatoes, mozzarella balls, and basil leaves onto cocktail picks to garnish.

VARIATION: DIRTY MARTINI

Add ½ teaspoon olive brine to the vodka in the cocktail shaker and garnish with a couple of pimiento-stuffed olives instead of the cherry tomatoes and mozzarella balls.

ESPRESSO MARTINI

YIELD: 1 COCKTAIL

I LOVE AN ESPRESSO MARTINI, BUT YOU CAN rarely get them sugar-free at a bar or restaurant, mostly because of different liqueurs mixologists like to use. Making them at home is delicious, and it's quite easy to remove the sugar. Using heavy cream as the finisher is the secret touch to marrying all the flavors together so you don't miss the sweet.

Ice cubes

2 ounces coffee bean–infused vodka (see page 36)

2 ounces espresso coffee or brewed coffee, cooled

1 ounce heavy cream

¼ teaspoon vanilla extract

3 whole coffee beans, for garnish

Fill a cocktail shaker with ice. Pour in the vodka, coffee, cream, and vanilla and shake until cold and frothy, 20–30 seconds. Strain into a martini glass and garnish with coffee beans.

WATERMELON MINT MARTINI

YIELD: 1 COCKTAIL

1 cup seedless watermelon chunks

Ice cubes

Juice of 1 lime, plus 1 lime wedge for garnish

1½ ounces vodka

Mint sprig, for garnish

Pinch smoked paprika, for garnish

WATERMELON YIELDS A LOT OF FRUIT, SO YOU could easily double or triple this recipe. I use cheesecloth to strain the watermelon pulp out of the cocktail, but you are welcome to use a blender and puree until smooth, leaving the pulp in.

Place the watermelon pieces in a large bowl lined with cheesecloth. Wrap the cheesecloth around the watermelon and squeeze all the juice into the bowl. Discard the pulp.

Fill a cocktail shaker with ice. Pour in the watermelon juice, lime juice, and vodka. Shake until cold, 15–20 seconds. Strain into a coupe and garnish with a lime wedge, mint sprig, and smoked paprika.

VILLA CAPPELLI OLIVE OIL MARTINI

YIELD: 1 COCKTAIL

- 3 fresh basil leaves
- Ice cubes
- 1½ ounces fresh grapefruit juice
- 1½ ounces vodka or gin
- 1 teaspoon Villa Cappelli olive oil
- 1 grapefruit peel, for garnish

IF YOU'VE LISTENED TO ME AT ALL OVER THE past 15 years, you know I've been obsessed with Villa Cappelli olive oil ever since I stayed at the villa in Terlizzi, Italy, in 2011 and became friends with the late, great Paul Cappelli. His surviving husband (and also a dear friend) Steven Crutchfield keeps the joint running, hosts people at the villa, and makes the liquid gold olive oil. If you ever plan a trip to Puglia, you must stay at Villa Cappelli and experience la dolce vita.

This cocktail is similar to a greyhound but elevated, and I've removed the simple syrup that Steven uses in his original recipe. You won't miss it if you get a sweet, in-season grapefruit.

From Steven: As you sip, the extra-virgin olive oil may begin to gently rise, creating a delicate golden layer atop your cocktail. This natural separation isn't just visual—it adds depth, enriching each sip with its silky texture and whisper of spice. The subtle aroma will linger while the oil kisses your lips.

Sigh.

Throw the basil leaves into the bottom of a cocktail shaker. Fill the shaker with ice. Add the grapefruit juice, vodka, and olive oil. Shake for 20–30 seconds to fully emulsify the olive oil. Strain into a martini glass, coupe, or Nick & Nora glass and garnish with the grapefruit peel.

THE VESPER

YIELD: 1 COCKTAIL

Ice cubes

1½ ounces vodka

1½ ounces gin

Dash orange bitters

1 lemon twist, for garnish

WHEN YOU CAN'T DECIDE BETWEEN GIN AND vodka, you make a vesper, which has the best of both worlds. A traditional vesper is made with ½ ounce Lillet Blanc, which is a floral orange blossom liqueur. But since we're omitting sugar, this recipe omits the Lillet and instead calls for a dash of orange bitters. Serve it ice cold, and garnish however you like. I go classic with a twist of lemon.

Fill a cocktail shaker with ice. Pour in the vodka, gin, and bitters. Shake for 20–30 seconds, until ice cold. Strain into a martini glass and garnish with the lemon twist.

THE VODKA SALAD

YIELD: 2 COCKTAILS

HERE'S A HANDY TRICK FOR ANY TIME YOU have extra herbs or citrus zest to use up: make a concentrate. The concentrate will last for up to a week in the fridge. It's a win-win, as you get a fun way to make your cocktails more interesting while using up stuff in the fridge.

I've been making a version of this cocktail for about 20 summers. I've always called it a vodka salad because so many green things go into it, it might as well be a serving of veggies for the day.

½ cup water

Grated zest and juice of 1 lime

4–5 fresh mint leaves, torn, plus whole leaves for garnish

3–4 fresh basil leaves, torn

Ice cubes

4 ounces vodka

1 tablespoon diced cucumber

Jalapeño slices, for garnish (optional)

Plain or lime-flavored soda water, to float

In a small saucepan, bring the water, lime zest, mint leaves, and basil leaves to a boil over medium heat. Lower the heat to medium-low and let simmer for 4–5 minutes, until slightly reduced. Strain the water into a mug or sturdy glass, discarding the herbs and zest. Let the extract chill in the fridge for 15–20 minutes.

Fill a shaker with ice. Pour in the concentrate, vodka, lime juice, and cucumber chunks and shake for 15–20 seconds, until ice cold. Strain into 2 ice-filled collins glasses. Float soda water to the top of each glass. Garnish with a few jalapeño slices and mint leaves.

THE SPICY SOUR

YIELD: 1 COCKTAIL

1 large egg white

Ice cubes for shaking, plus one large ice cube for serving

1 ounce jalapeño-infused gin (see page 36)

1 ounce gin

1 ounce fresh blood orange juice

2–3 strawberries, muddled well or pureed in a blender or small food processor

Plain soda water, to float

1 jalapeño slice, for garnish

WHAT MAKES THIS COCKTAIL SPICY IS HOME-made jalapeño-infused gin. You will only use a bit of the infused gin and cut it with regular gin. But feel free to add more infused gin if you love spicy!

If blood oranges aren't available, you can use a regular orange for this recipe.

Pour the egg white into a dry cocktail shaker, then cover and shake vigorously for 20–30 seconds, until the egg white is frothy. Add ice to the shaker, then add the infused gin, regular gin, blood orange juice, and strawberry puree. Shake to blend for 15–20 seconds. Strain into a rocks glass with one large ice cube, float soda water to fill the glass, and garnish with the jalapeño slice.

MAMA'S FANCY MOCKTAIL

YIELD: 2 MOCKTAILS

YOU DON'T NEED ALCOHOL TO BE FANCY. JUST grab some gorgeous blood orange juice, soda water, and a couple of champagne flutes and you've got yourself a bubbly treat that everyone will envy. Blood oranges are in season only once a year, but now you can find bottled blood orange juice in some produce fridges or even on the shelves of some natural grocers.

Ice cubes

2 ounces fresh blood orange juice

2 ounces fresh lime juice

Plain soda water, to float

Fill a cocktail shaker with ice. Pour in the blood orange juice and lime juice and shake for 15–20 seconds, until ice cold. Strain into two champagne flutes and top with soda water.

MOJITO MOCKTAIL

YIELD: 1 MOCKTAIL

- 3–4 fresh raspberries, plus more for garnish
- 3–4 fresh strawberries, chopped, plus whole berries for garnish
- 7–10 fresh mint leaves, plus 1 mint sprig for garnish
- 1 lime, cut into 4 wedges
- Ice cubes
- Plain soda water, to float

WHILE A REGULAR MOJITO IS MADE WITH light rum, and we might even infuse that rum with mint leaves for extra minty goodness, here we make a mocktail with no added sugar so that everyone can enjoy the nonalcoholic version of this classic cocktail.

In a small bowl, muddle the raspberries, strawberries, several mint leaves, and the juice of 2 lime wedges. Pour through a strainer, using the muddler to push it through the strainer into a highball or collins glass. Fill the glass with ice, then float soda water to the top of the glass, leaving room to garnish with the prettiest of the berries, a giant mint sprig, and the remaining 2 lime wedges.

Whipped Guac with Lime-Infused Olive Oil, page 111

DIPS

DILL PICKLE RANCH DIP

YIELD: 1½ CUPS

1 cup sour cream

3 tablespoons goat cheese

2 tablespoons dill pickle juice

1 tablespoon fresh lemon juice

1 teaspoon onion powder

1 teaspoon garlic powder

1 teaspoon minced fresh dill, plus more for garnish

½ teaspoon dried dill

½ teaspoon salt

½ teaspoon pepper

2 dill pickles, finely chopped (about ½ cup)

WE ARE 'MURICAN. WE LOVE RANCH. WE LOVE pickles. We love them all together. When I make this, I save a few steps and use Eat Happy Kitchen Ranch Dust in place of the onion powder, garlic powder, dried dill, salt, and pepper. The dip is delish with cut raw veggies or Sour Cream Ranch Crackers (page 131).

In a mixing bowl, stir together the sour cream, goat cheese, dill pickle juice, lemon juice, onion powder, garlic powder, fresh dill, dried dill, salt, and pepper until well mixed and smooth. Fold in the chopped dill pickles. Transfer the dip to a serving bowl. Garnish with additional fresh dill.

GREEN CHILI QUESO DIP WITH CHORIZO

YIELD: 3 CUPS

SOUTH OF THE BORDER IN TEXAS, THERE'S A little joint called Torchy's Tacos, and I am obsessed. I stop at the Waco Torchy's halfway through my drive from Dallas to Austin every time I am doing a tour of Central Market to promote Eat Happy Kitchen pasta sauces. Last time I was there, I told the staff that I came all the way from California for their queso dip, which is very much true. They were shocked that I eat it with a spoon instead of with the corn chips they tried to serve me. You don't need corn chips, friends. I created my version of this perfect dip here for you, so get your spoons ready. If you must have something to dip in your dip, use cut veggies or my Tortilla Chips (page 136), Hot Crackers (page 132), or Sour Cream Ranch Crackers (page 131).

- 1 (8-ounce) package cream cheese, at room temperature
- ¼ cup heavy cream
- 1 cup Lime Green Salsa (page 100) or store-bought green salsa
- 2 cups freshly grated mild cheddar cheese
- 2 cups freshly grated Monterey Jack cheese
- 2 garlic cloves, minced
- 2 teaspoons no-sugar-added hot sauce
- ½ teaspoon ground cumin
- 1 (6-ounce) can diced Hatch green chiles, drained
- 4 ounces chorizo, browned
- ½ avocado, peeled and cubed
- 2 ounces cotija or queso fresco, crumbled
- 1 tablespoon chopped fresh tomato
- 1 teaspoon chopped fresh cilantro leaves
- 4–5 jalapeño slices

In a large saucepan or Dutch oven, bring the cream cheese, cream, and salsa to a low boil over medium heat, whisking frequently to make sure the mixture doesn't scald and to break up any lumps in the cream cheese. Incorporate the cheddar and Monterey Jack cheeses in batches, melting the cheese evenly with each handful you add. Stir in the garlic, hot sauce, and cumin. Fold in the chiles.

Transfer the dip to a serving bowl and garnish with the chorizo, avocado, cotija, tomato, cilantro, and jalapeño slices. Serve immediately.

LIME GREEN SALSA

YIELD: 2 CUPS

1½ pounds tomatillos, husked and rinsed

1 (6-ounce) can chopped Hatch green chiles, with their juices

Juice of 1 lime

¼ sweet onion

¼ cup fresh cilantro leaves

PUT THIS SALSA RECIPE IN YOUR ARSENAL, AND you will have a party ready to go. Plus you can use it with tacos, enchiladas, or for serving with pan-fried halloumi cheese or queso panelo. Bonus points if you fire-roast the tomatillos on the grill on an open flame instead of roasting them in the oven, but it's deliciously addictive no matter how you make it. Just make it.

Preheat the oven to 350 degrees F. Line a rimmed baking sheet with parchment paper.

Place the tomatillos on the lined baking sheet and bake for 20–30 minutes, until soft and slightly seared. Remove from the oven and let cool for at least 10–15 minutes.

In a high-speed blender, combine the roasted tomatillos, chiles, lime juice, onion, and cilantro leaves and pulse to reach the desired consistency, 15–20 seconds.

FRENCH ONION DIP

YIELD: 2 CUPS

EVERY FOOTBALL SUNDAY, MY MOM WOULD dip Utz potato chips into sour cream mixed with Lipton onion soup mix. It's a flavor I've been chasing my whole life. I've found that the flavors can be replicated when we make that dip from scratch, giving us the yum without all the processed ingredients and sugar. Serve alongside Sour Cream Ranch Crackers (page 131) or cut raw veggies.

- 1 tablespoon olive oil
- 2 large shallots, thinly sliced
- 1 sweet onion, thinly sliced
- Salt and pepper
- 1 tablespoon white wine vinegar
- 1 (8-ounce) package cream cheese, at room temperature
- 1 cup sour cream
- 1/2 teaspoon garlic powder
- 1/2 teaspoon onion powder
- 1/2 cup whole milk, or more if needed
- Chopped fresh chives, for garnish

Heat the olive oil in a large, flat-bottomed sauté pan over medium-high heat. Toss the shallots and onion in the oil and season them with salt and pepper. Lower the heat to medium and cover the pan to sweat the shallots and onion for 7–8 minutes. Remove the lid and toss the shallots and onion, then continue to cook until they start to brown, another 3–4 minutes. Sprinkle in the white wine vinegar and continue cooking until caramelized, about 20 minutes. Remove from the heat and let cool for 10 minutes. Chop the shallots and onion and set aside.

In a large mixing bowl, beat the cream cheese with a hand mixer until fluffy. Add the sour cream, garlic powder, and onion powder and beat until mixed. Season with salt and pepper. Fold in half the caramelized shallots and onion and thin out with the milk to your desired consistency. Pour the dip into a serving bowl, then garnish with the remaining caramelized shallots and onion and fresh chives.

CREAMY MUSHROOM DIP

YIELD: 2½ CUPS

8 ounces whole cremini (baby bella) mushrooms

1 tablespoon olive oil

½ sweet onion, minced

Salt and pepper

¼ teaspoon garlic powder

¼ teaspoon onion powder

2 garlic cloves, minced

1 tablespoon red wine vinegar

½ cup sour cream

¼ cup Boursin cheese

4 ounces cream cheese, at room temperature

½ cup fresh mozzarella, finely chopped

¼ cup freshly grated Parmesan cheese

Chopped fresh parsley, for garnish

THE EARTHINESS AND SAVORINESS OF MUSHrooms has always been one of my favorite taste sensations. Turning them into a creamy dip is a no-brainer. Eat this on its own, serve it as an app, or you can even use it as a topping for roasted chicken or grilled steak. As a dip, it is lovely alongside Sour Cream Ranch Crackers (page 131), veggie slices, or Tortilla Chips (page 136).

Preheat the oven to 400 degrees F.

Remove the stems from the mushrooms, cutting off and discarding the rough ends. Finely chop the remaining stems and thinly slice the caps.

Heat the olive oil in a large, flat-bottomed sauté pan over medium-high heat until shimmering. Add the onion and cook for 1–2 minutes, until the onion becomes slightly translucent. Add the mushrooms and cook for 5–6 minutes without stirring to get a good sear. Season well with salt and pepper, then sprinkle on the garlic powder and onion powder. Stir in the minced garlic and cook for 2–3 more minutes, until the mushrooms are cooked through. Sprinkle on the red wine vinegar and let the pan sizzle for a minute, then reduce the heat to medium-low. Fold in the sour cream, Boursin cheese, and cream cheese until softened and evenly mixed. Fold in the mozzarella until melted and incorporated.

Transfer the contents of the pan to a small casserole dish. Evenly sprinkle the Parmesan on top. Bake for 20 minutes, until the top is golden brown. Remove from the oven and garnish with chopped parsley.

SLOW-COOKED RANCH CHICKEN DIP

YIELD: 6–8 SERVINGS

IN COOLER WEATHER, I LOVE TO THROW chicken in a slow cooker; it makes for nicely juicy, shreddable chicken that can be used in a variety of recipes. Here, we're adding cheese and ranch for the ultimate rich comfort food, perfect for an ugly sweater party or any football game. Serve alongside Sour Cream Ranch Crackers (page 131), Hot Crackers (page 132), and/or sliced veggies.

1–2 pounds boneless, skinless chicken thighs or breasts (or a combination)

Salt and pepper

1 sweet onion, chopped

2 tablespoons Eat Happy Kitchen Ranch Dust or other natural ranch seasoning

2 (8-ounce) packages cream cheese, cubed

8 slices bacon

2 cups freshly grated sharp cheddar cheese

1 tablespoon chopped fresh chives

Season the chicken lightly with salt and pepper. Arrange the chicken and chopped onion in a 4-quart slow cooker. Evenly sprinkle the ranch seasoning over the chicken and onion. Scatter the cream cheese cubes over the top. Cover and cook on low for 5–6 hours.

Close to the end of the slow cooker cook time, preheat the oven to 400 degrees F. Line a rimmed baking sheet with aluminum foil or parchment paper.

Lay the bacon slices on the lined baking sheet and bake for 15–20 minutes, until crispy. Remove from the oven and drain on a paper towel–lined plate. Chop the cooked bacon into small crumbles.

Shred the chicken with two forks or culinary claws. Add the chopped bacon and top with the cheddar cheese. Place the cover back on the slow cooker and cook for 15–20 minutes, until the cheese has melted. Garnish the dip with the chives.

BAKED BRIE

YIELD: 1 (6-INCH) BAKED BRIE

- 1 tablespoon pine nuts
- 3 tablespoons salted butter, divided
- 3 tablespoons minced shallot
- ¼ cup dried cranberries
- 1 tablespoon white wine vinegar
- ⅔ cup almond flour or crushed pork rinds
- ½ teaspoon baking powder
- ½ teaspoon salt, plus more for seasoning
- ½ teaspoon garlic powder
- ½ teaspoon onion powder
- 1½ cups freshly grated Colby Jack cheese
- 3 tablespoons cream cheese, at room temperature
- 1 large egg
- Olive oil
- 1 (4- to 6-inch) Brie wheel, at room temperature

BAKED BRIE IS SUCH A LUXURY AND IS JUST about always made with puff pastry or phyllo dough . . . so that means carbs and gluten. Here's a low-carb version that feels just as luxurious without all the extra stuff we don't need.

I recommend cooking this in a small casserole dish to contain all the goodness and keep it from oozing out onto a baking sheet. Then you can use a serving knife to cut the baked brie and its low-carb shell to spread onto sliced apples, pears, low-carb crackers, or veggies.

Preheat the oven to 400 degrees F.

In a small sauté pan, toast the pine nuts over medium heat until fragrant and starting to brown, about 3 minutes. Transfer the pine nuts to a paper towel. Add 1 tablespoon of the butter to the same pan and let it melt and start to bubble. Add the shallot and cranberries and let them soften for 4–5 minutes, stirring frequently. Add the vinegar—it will sizzle! Cook for 2–3 minutes, until the shallot starts to caramelize. Turn the heat down to low if it starts to burn. Remove the pan from the heat and let stand while making the pastry shell.

In a mixing bowl, whisk together the almond flour, baking powder, salt, garlic powder, and onion powder, then add the Colby Jack cheese, cream cheese, and egg. Stir just until a dough ball forms, but do not overmix.

Line a small casserole dish with parchment paper. Drizzle some olive oil onto your fingertips and press the dough ball onto the parchment paper to about ¼-inch

thickness. Place the Brie wheel in the center of the pastry dough. Pour all but 1 tablespoon of the shallot-cranberry mixture on top of the Brie wheel, and sprinkle all but 1 teaspoon of the toasted pine nuts on top. Season with salt, then fold the pastry over the sides and top of the Brie wheel and gently press the top flat to seal it off.

Bake for 13–15 minutes, or until golden brown on top. Remove from the oven and let stand for 5 minutes. Meanwhile, melt the remaining 2 tablespoons butter. Brush the top of the wrapped Brie with melted butter and garnish with the remaining shallot-cranberry mixture and pine nuts. Serve hot in the casserole dish.

WHIPPED GUAC
WITH LIME-INFUSED OLIVE OIL

YIELD: 2 CUPS

MAKE THE LIME-INFUSED OLIVE OIL THE DAY before making the guac for the optimal infusion of lime flavor. The extra acid from the lime-infused olive oil and the swirl of blood orange juice add layers of flavor to the guacamole, cutting the richness of the avocado in the best possible way. Plus, if you can find a blood orange in season, the color added to the top of this dip makes it feel extra party-ready. This guac is delicious with cut veggies or my Tortilla Chips (page 136).

3 tablespoons olive oil

Strips of peel and juice of 1 lime

4 perfectly ripe avocados, pitted and peeled

Salt and pepper

¼ cup chopped cherry tomatoes, plus more for garnish

2 tablespoons chopped fresh cilantro leaves, plus more for garnish

2 tablespoons chopped jalapeños (include the seeds if you like the heat)

Juice of 1 blood orange or regular orange

Pour the olive oil into a small glass and drop in the lime peel. Cover and let it infuse at room temperature for 2 hours, or in the fridge for up to a day.

In a medium mixing bowl, season the avocados with salt and pepper. Add the tomatoes, cilantro, jalapeños, and lime juice. Using a hand mixer on the medium setting, whip all the ingredients until smooth, 30–60 seconds. Season once more to taste with salt and pepper.

Transfer the guac to a serving bowl and smooth out the surface, leaving a couple of troughs. Drizzle the lime-infused olive oil into the troughs, then drizzle the blood orange juice over the olive oil. Garnish with extra chopped cherry tomatoes and cilantro leaves, and season once more with salt.

EIGHT-LAYER DIP

YIELD: 8–10 SERVINGS

1 pound ground beef (I use 85% lean)

2 tablespoons Eat Happy Kitchen Taco Dust Seasoning or other no-sugar-added taco seasoning

¼ cup water

1 (15-ounce) can black beans or pinto beans, rinsed and drained

½ teaspoon salt

½ teaspoon ground cumin

1 cup sour cream

½ cup salsa

1 cup chopped romaine lettuce

Whipped Guac with Lime-Infused Olive Oil (page 111) or store-bought guacamole

1 cup crumbled queso fresco

Sliced jalapeños, for garnish

Chopped tomato, for garnish

Chopped fresh cilantro, for garnish

WE'RE ALL FAMILIAR WITH SEVEN-LAYER DIP, but this dip is one louder.

You can serve this dip in a giant bowl, or make individual dip cups, which is a fun way to allow people to keep their dip all to themselves. Premade taco seasoning is a handy shortcut for flavoring the beef, but be sure to check the label—some seasoning blends have lurking sugar. Or just use Eat Happy Kitchen Taco Dust Seasoning! Serve with chopped veggies or Hot Crackers (page 132).

Heat a large sauté pan over medium-high heat. Add the ground beef and cook, breaking it up and crumbling it with a spatula, until fully cooked and browned, about 5 minutes. Remove from the heat and add the taco seasoning and water. (If you like, you can first drain off the beef fat from the pan, but I like to use it to help the taco seasoning blend into the beef.) Stir until the beef is coated in seasoning.

In a bowl, season the black beans with the salt and cumin.

In a large serving bowl or an 8 x 8-inch glass baking dish, assemble the following layers in this order: sour cream, beef, salsa, lettuce, beans, guacamole, and queso fresco. Top the dip with jalapeño slices, chopped tomato, and cilantro. (Alternatively, to make individual dip cups, layer 2 tablespoons of each component into each cup.)

CREAMY BEET HUMMUS

YIELD: 2 CUPS

BEET HUMMUS IS BY FAR THE PRETTIEST HUMmus ever. And since any kind of hummus is easy to make, this recipe is a no-brainer. The addition of soft cream cheese makes for an extra smooth hummus texture that pairs beautifully with crunchy Tortilla Chips (page 136) or cut veggies.

- 1 (15-ounce) can chickpeas, rinsed and drained
- ½ cup cooked, ready-to-eat beets
- ⅓ cup tahini
- 2 ounces cream cheese, at room temperature
- 1 teaspoon minced garlic
- 1 tablespoon lemon juice
- 1 teaspoon salt
- ½ teaspoon pepper
- ⅓ cup plus 1 tablespoon olive oil, plus more for drizzling
- 1 teaspoon minced lemon zest
- 2 tablespoons chopped fresh parsley
- 2 tablespoons roasted pistachios, crushed
- 1 teaspoon harissa seasoning blend

Combine the chickpeas, beets, tahini, cream cheese, garlic, lemon juice, salt, and pepper in a food processor or high-speed blender and blend until smooth, 15–20 seconds. Then pulse the hummus while continuously drizzling in ⅓ cup of the olive oil through the feed tube to incorporate.

In a small mixing bowl, mix the remaining 1 tablespoon olive oil, the lemon zest, parsley, pistachios, and harissa.

Transfer the beet hummus to a serving bowl and garnish with the topping mixture and an extra drizzle of olive oil.

ROMESCO SOUP SHOTS

YIELD: 2½ CUPS (6–8 SOUP SHOTS)

- 2 cups cherry tomatoes or other small tomatoes
- 4 garlic cloves, halved
- 2 tablespoons olive oil, plus more for drizzling
- Salt and pepper
- ½ cup jarred roasted red bell peppers, drained (or homemade and peeled)
- ¼ cup almonds
- ½ teaspoon smoked paprika
- 2 tablespoons mayonnaise or Greek yogurt (optional)

I WISH MORE RESTAURANTS SERVED SHOTS OF soup. That way you could try the soup of the day without getting too full for dinner. I serve soup shots as a fun amuse-bouche at my dinner parties. Romesco sauce is a traditional Catalan sauce that is amazing with fish or chicken. I love it so much I turned it into its own soup (shot) for you to try. While you can just shoot your shot, it is also excellent as a personal dip for cut raw veggies or crackers.

Preheat the oven to 375 degrees F. Line a rimmed baking sheet with parchment paper.

Spread the cherry tomatoes and garlic cloves on the lined baking sheet. Drizzle them with olive oil and season with salt and pepper. Roast for 15–20 minutes, until the tomatoes are soft, blistered, and starting to char. Remove from the oven and let cool for 10–15 minutes.

Transfer the roasted tomatoes, garlic, and any juices from the baking sheet into a high-speed blender or mini food processor. Add the roasted red bell peppers, almonds, smoked paprika, olive oil, salt, pepper, and the mayonnaise, if desired. Blend until pureed and smooth. Pour into shot glasses and garnish with additional pepper.

MEDITERRANEAN BAKED FETA DIP

YIELD: 4–6 SERVINGS

THE SAVORY FLAVORS OF THIS DIP ARE ADDICtive. While feta isn't the creamiest when baked, you can slice it up into pieces so that folks can dip their veggie slices or low-carb crackers and build the perfect bite for themselves. Add the basil just before serving to keep the leaves green, fresh, and flavorful.

- Olive oil, for drizzling
- 1 (8-ounce) block feta cheese
- ½ red onion, sliced
- 6 mini bell peppers, seeded and thinly sliced lengthwise
- ⅓ cup cherry tomatoes, halved
- ¼ cup chopped sun-dried tomatoes
- ½ cup whole pitted kalamata olives
- Salt and pepper
- Fresh basil leaves, for garnish

Preheat the oven to 400 degrees F.

Drizzle the bottom of an 8 x 8-inch baking dish with olive oil. Place the feta square in the center. Scatter the onion, bell pepper, cherry tomatoes, sun-dried tomatoes, and olives around the feta. Season just the veggies around the feta with salt and pepper. Drizzle more olive oil atop the veggies and feta.

Bake for 1 hour, or until the veggies are soft and blistered and the feta is soft and starting to turn golden. Remove from the oven, drizzle the feta with additional olive oil, and top with fresh basil leaves.

SMOKED SALMON BOARD

YIELD: 6–8 SERVINGS

- 16 ounces whipped cream cheese
- 1 tablespoon minced lemon zest, plus 1 tablespoon lemon juice
- 8 ounces smoked salmon, torn into small pieces
- 2 tablespoons drained capers
- ¼ cup chopped red onion
- Olive oil, for drizzling
- Lemon wedges, for serving

A FEW YEARS AGO, BUTTER BOARDS SWEPT the socials, but here's what I find to be a more useful board: the smoked salmon board. It's a perfect starter for a lovely brunch, or a great addition to a table of apps at a classy party. Instead of having to make individual bites, you put it all on the board and serve with a side of veggies or low-carb crackers.

In a mixing bowl, stir together the whipped cream cheese, lemon zest, and lemon juice until smooth. Scoop dollops of the lemon cream cheese onto a serving platter in a wide circle, close to the outer edge of the platter. Using the back side of the spoon, press the dollops into shallow indentations. Place torn pieces of smoked salmon in each indentation. Repeat, making inner rings of lemon cream cheese and smoked salmon until the platter is covered. Sprinkle on the capers and onion, then drizzle olive oil across the platter. Serve with lemon wedges.

Mini Taco Cups, *page 143*

BITES

SESAME DEVILED EGGS

YIELD: 24 DEVILED EGGS

- 1 large shallot, minced
- ¼ cup red wine vinegar
- Whole spices, such as star anise, whole cloves, allspice berries, and peppercorns
- 12 large eggs, hard-boiled for 10 minutes (see headnote), cooled, peeled, and halved
- ¼ cup sour cream
- 2 tablespoons Dijon mustard
- 1 tablespoon plus 1 teaspoon gluten-free soy sauce or coconut aminos
- ½ teaspoon sriracha, plus more for garnish (optional)
- 1 teaspoon cold-pressed toasted sesame oil
- White and black sesame seeds, for garnish

DEVILED EGGS ARE THE PERFECT PARTY FOOD. They are the first thing to get eaten the moment the tray is set out on the table. This version is a fun twist on a classic. You might even want to make double the pickled shallots because they complement the richness of the eggs so well; note that you'll need to pickle the shallot the night before you make the eggs, so plan ahead.

My foolproof hard-boiled egg method: Bring a pot of water to a full boil over high heat, add the eggs and boil for 10 minutes, then use a ladle to transfer the eggs to an ice bath to cool quickly. Peel the eggs in the ice bath, then dry them off. Voilà, you are ready to devil some eggs!

Place the minced shallot in a small ramekin and cover with the vinegar and a few of your favorite whole spices. Refrigerate overnight. Drain and discard the vinegar and spices. Reserve the shallot for serving.

Carefully pop the cooked yolks out of the egg white halves into a large mixing bowl. Using a hand mixer, combine the egg yolks, sour cream, mustard, soy sauce, sriracha, and sesame oil until smooth and creamy. Scrape the yolk mixture into a piping bag (fitted with a star tip, if you're feeling extra fancy). If you don't have a piping bag, you can use a resealable plastic bag. Just scoop the yolk mixture into the bag, seal, and press the contents toward one of the bottom corners of the bag. Snip off the corner of the bag with scissors.

Set the empty egg white halves on a platter. Scoop ⅛ teaspoon minced shallot into the bottom of each egg white. Pipe the yolk mixture evenly into the egg white halves over the shallot. Top with an additional ⅛ teaspoon shallot and a drop of sriracha (optional). Sprinkle the sesame seeds on top. Keep chilled until ready to serve.

BABY BLATS WITH HOMEMADE THOUSAND ISLAND DRESSING

YIELD: 12 BABY BLATS AND 1 CUP DRESSING

THINK OF THIS AS A SLIDER VERSION OF A BLAT (bacon, lettuce, avocado, and tomato), using a hard-boiled egg for the BLAT bun. Use toothpicks or cocktail picks to hold these together if needed. For perfect hard-boiled eggs, see headnote on page 124.

THOUSAND ISLAND DRESSING

¾ cup mayonnaise

2 tablespoons no-sugar-added ketchup

1 garlic clove, minced

1 tablespoon no-sugar-added hot sauce

2 tablespoons minced sweet onion

½ dill pickle spear, chopped

BABY BLATS

12 large eggs, hard-boiled (see page 124), cooled, peeled, and halved

8–10 bacon slices, cooked until crispy and cut into 2-inch pieces

3 small tomatoes, thinly sliced

Butter lettuce, torn into small pieces

1 avocado, pitted, peeled, and thinly sliced

Pepper

Minced dried onion flakes, for garnish

Whisk together all the dressing ingredients for a chunky dressing, or use a food processor or blender to mix for a smooth dressing. Set aside.

To make your egg "buns": On 12 of the egg halves, slice off a sliver from the rounded outside of the egg; this creates a flat bottom surface so your BLAT will stand upright when assembled.

Place the bottom halves on a platter. Add some dressing, bacon, a tomato slice, lettuce, and avocado, and top with the other half of the egg. Attach with a toothpick to hold it together. Season with pepper and a sprinkle of onion flakes. Serve immediately.

CLOUD BREAD SPINACH BITES

YIELDS 2 CUPS SPINACH DIP AND ABOUT 36 CLOUD BREAD ROUNDS

HOT SPINACH DIP

1 tablespoon olive oil

½ sweet onion, minced

1 (10-ounce) bag frozen spinach, thawed and pressed dry

2 cups packed fresh spinach, loosely chopped

Salt and pepper

¼ teaspoon garlic powder

¼ teaspoon onion powder

⅛ teaspoon ground nutmeg

¼ cup almond flour

¼ cup heavy cream

¾ cup grated Gruyère cheese

1 teaspoon no-sugar-added hot sauce (optional)

Freshly grated Parmesan cheese, for garnish

CLOUD BREAD MINI ROUNDS

6 large egg whites

¼ teaspoon cream of tartar

½ cup cottage cheese

2 tablespoons sour cream

½ teaspoon salt

¼ teaspoon baking soda

THESE TASTY SPINACH BITES ARE GREAT FOR brunch. They have the same eggy, cheesy appeal of mini quiches, but without the carby crust. If you're not a fan of spinach dip, the cloud bread mini rounds make an excellent base for all sorts of canapés, so feel free to get creative with your toppings.

Preheat the oven to 325 degrees F. Line a rimmed baking sheet with parchment paper.

Heat the olive oil in a large, flat-bottomed sauté pan over medium-high heat. Add the onion and cook until soft, 2–3 minutes. Add the frozen and fresh spinach and cook for 2–3 minutes, until the fresh spinach is completely wilted. Season with salt and pepper, then stir in the garlic powder, onion powder, and nutmeg. Mix in the almond flour, followed by the heavy cream. Fold in the Gruyère cheese and optional hot sauce, then remove the pan from the heat and set aside.

Using a standing mixer or electric hand mixer on high, whip the egg whites and cream of tartar in a glass or metal bowl to very stiff peaks.

In a smaller glass bowl, whip the cottage cheese and sour cream until soft. It will not get totally smooth, but most of the large curds from the cottage cheese should be smoothed out. Gently stir the salt and baking soda into the cottage cheese mixture. Fold the cheese mixture into the egg whites until blended but not overmixed.

Scoop the batter into a pastry bag. If you don't have one, use a resealable plastic bag and snip off the bottom corner. Pipe the batter in 1½-inch buttons onto the prepared baking sheet, 2–3 inches apart. Bake for 8–10 minutes, until cooked through and golden brown. Remove from the oven.

Drain off any excess liquid that has formed in the pan of spinach dip. Gently scoop a small spoonful of the spinach dip onto each cloud bread round. Top each bite with grated Parmesan. Return the sheet to the oven for 5 more minutes, or until the Parmesan starts to turn golden brown. Remove from the oven and let stand for 5 minutes before serving.

SOUR CREAM RANCH CRACKERS

YIELD: 30–40 CRACKERS

THIS RECIPE AND MY HOT CRACKERS (PAGE 132) are variations on a low-carb cracker. Feel free to change up the flavor profiles however you can think of, or make them as is for the perfect complement to any of the dip recipes in this book. You can use 1 tablespoon Eat Happy Kitchen Ranch Dust in place of the dill, onion powder, garlic powder, salt, and pepper.

- 1½ cups almond flour
- 1 teaspoon dried dill weed
- ½ teaspoon onion powder
- ½ teaspoon garlic powder
- ½ teaspoon salt
- ¼ teaspoon freshly ground black pepper
- ¼ cup sour cream

Preheat the oven to 350 degrees F.

In a large mixing bowl, whisk together the almond flour, dill, onion powder, garlic powder, salt, and pepper. Add the sour cream and use a fork or your hands to blend the ingredients until you create a dough ball.

Transfer the dough ball to a large piece of parchment paper. Cover the dough with another piece of parchment. Use a rolling pin to roll the dough between the two pieces of parchment to ¼-inch thickness, as evenly as possible. Gently remove the top piece of parchment and discard. Cut the dough into 1¼-inch squares—a pizza cutter comes in handy for this. Or, if you'd like your crackers to be fun shapes, use a cookie cutter.

Transfer the parchment and crackers to a rimmed baking sheet. Bake for 7–8 minutes, until golden brown. Remove from the oven and let cool on the baking sheet for at least 5–10 minutes to crisp up. Serve right away or store in an airtight container at room temperature for up to 4 days.

HOT CRACKERS

YIELD: 30–40 CRACKERS

1½ cups almond flour

½ teaspoon salt, plus more for seasoning

½ teaspoon onion powder

½ teaspoon garlic powder

½ teaspoon red pepper flakes

¼ teaspoon cayenne pepper

¼ cup sour cream

Olive oil, for brushing

THESE SPICY LOW-CARB CRACKERS ARE A terrific accompaniment to so many of the dips in this book. Want to crank up the heat? Add more ground cayenne and red pepper flakes. Rolling these out as thinly as you can ensures that they crisp up nicely.

Preheat the oven to 350 degrees F.

In a large mixing bowl, whisk together the almond flour, salt, onion powder, garlic powder, red pepper flakes, and cayenne. Add the sour cream and use a fork or your hands to blend the ingredients until you create a dough ball.

Transfer the dough ball to a large piece of parchment paper. Cover the dough with another piece of parchment. Use a rolling pin to roll the dough between the two pieces of parchment to ¼-inch thickness, as evenly as possible. Gently remove the top piece of parchment and discard. Cut the dough into 1¼-inch squares (or triangles if you're making the Spicy Pizza Bites on page 135)—a pizza cutter comes in handy for this. Or, if you'd like your crackers to be fun shapes, use a cookie cutter.

Transfer the parchment paper and crackers to a rimmed baking sheet. Bake for 7–8 minutes, until golden brown. Remove from the oven, lightly brush the crackers with olive oil, lightly season with salt, and let them cool on the baking sheet for at least 5–10 minutes to crisp up. Serve right away or store in an airtight container at room temperature for up to 4 days.

SPICY PIZZA BITES

YIELD: 30–35 PIZZA BITES

BACK IN MY GLUTEN AND CARB DAYS, I LOVED a cracker-thin pizza crust. We can easily achieve legend cracker crust status by using the recipe for Hot Crackers (page 132) as crispy, super thin pizza bites. I love the cracker-crust pizza vibes without breaking the carb bank.

- 1 recipe Hot Crackers (page 132), cut into triangles
- Freshly grated mozzarella cheese
- Chopped pepperoni
- Dried oregano
- Eat Happy Kitchen Arrabbiata Spicy Marinara Sauce or your favorite brand with no added sugar, warmed, for dipping

Preheat an air fryer or oven to 350 degrees F. If using the oven, line a rimmed baking sheet with parchment paper.

To air-fry: Working in batches as necessary, arrange a single layer of cracker triangles in the air fryer basket. Top each cracker with a little mozzarella, pepperoni, and a sprinkle of dried oregano. Air-fry for 3 minutes. Remove from the air fryer and serve hot with the dipping sauce.

To bake: Arrange a single layer of cracker triangles on the lined baking sheet. Top each cracker with a little mozzarella, pepperoni, and a sprinkle of dried oregano. Bake for 3–4 minutes, or until the cheese is melted. Remove from the oven and serve hot with the dipping sauce.

TORTILLA CHIPS

YIELD: 14–16 CHIPS

- 1½ cups freshly grated Colby Jack cheese
- ½ cup almond flour
- 2 tablespoons coconut flour
- 1 teaspoon salt
- ½ teaspoon baking powder
- ½ teaspoon paprika
- ½ teaspoon garlic powder
- ¼ teaspoon ground cumin

THESE TORTILLA CHIPS ARE SIMPLE TO MAKE, but the geometry of cutting them may be a challenge. It was for me. The key is to cut diagonal, crisscrossing lines to create large diamond shapes, and then cut the diamonds into triangles. My ninth-grade geometry teacher would be so proud of me. Serve these chips alongside Whipped Guac (page 111), Eight-Layer Dip (page 112), Creamy Beet Hummus (page 115), Green Chili Queso Dip (page 99), or whatever your heart desires.

Preheat the oven to 350 degrees F.

Put the cheese in a microwave-safe mixing bowl and microwave for 30–45 seconds, or until the cheese is soft and pliable and starting to release some of its oil.

In another mixing bowl, whisk together the almond flour, coconut flour, salt, baking powder, paprika, garlic powder, and cumin. Pour the dry ingredients into the melted cheese and stir well to incorporate into a smooth dough.

Transfer the dough to a large piece of parchment paper. Cover the dough with another piece of parchment. Use a rolling pin to roll the dough between the two pieces of parchment to ⅛-inch thickness, or as thin as possible without breakage. Gently remove the top piece of parchment and discard. Using a pizza cutter or knife, cut the dough into triangle shapes.

Transfer the parchment paper and chips to a rimmed baking sheet. Bake for 5–7 minutes, or until the chips are starting to turn golden brown. Remove from the oven and let cool completely.

LOW-CARB "RAVIOLI" BITES

YIELD: 22–25 "RAVIOLI"

MINI RAVIOLI—DONE LOW CARB? REALLY, THEY are just meatballs wrapped in melted provolone. And yet, it works in both presentation and flavor. Use your desired fat content ground beef; I usually default to 85 percent lean, as that's widely available in stores.

- 8 ounces ground pork
- 8 ounces ground beef
- 2 teaspoons yellow mustard
- 1/4 cup almond flour
- 1 large egg
- 1 teaspoon minced fresh parsley
- 1 teaspoon salt
- 1/2 teaspoon pepper
- 1/2 teaspoon dried oregano, plus more for garnish
- 1/2 teaspoon dried basil, plus more for garnish
- 1/2 teaspoon garlic powder
- 1/2 teaspoon onion powder
- 12–14 provolone cheese slices, cut into quarters
- Eat Happy Kitchen Marinara Sauce or your favorite brand with no added sugar, warmed, for dipping

Preheat the oven to 350 degrees F. Line a rimmed baking sheet with parchment paper.

In a large mixing bowl, combine the pork, beef, mustard, almond flour, egg, parsley, salt, pepper, oregano, basil, garlic powder, and onion powder. Using your hands, blend well, then form into 1-inch meatballs. Place the meatballs on the lined baking sheet. Bake for 15 minutes. Remove from the oven and transfer the meatballs to a paper towel–lined plate to drain any excess drippings.

Line the baking sheet with a fresh sheet of parchment. To make each "ravioli," layer one piece of cheese, one meatball, and then a second piece of cheese on top, spacing the "ravioli" at least 2 inches apart.

Bake for 5–7 minutes. Remove from the oven and let cool for 5 minutes, until the ravioli are easily removed from the baking sheet. If the cheese has melted too far away from the meatball, use a spatula to tuck the cheese back against the meatball to give it a ravioli shape. Garnish with a sprinkle of dried oregano and basil. Serve with marinara for dipping.

JALAPEÑO CHEDDAR MINI MUFFINS

YIELD: 24 MINI MUFFINS

- Avocado, coconut, or olive oil nonstick spray
- ¼ cup almond flour
- ¼ cup coconut flour
- ½ teaspoon baking powder
- ½ teaspoon salt
- ¼ teaspoon onion powder
- ¼ teaspoon garlic powder
- 4 tablespoons salted butter, melted, plus more butter for serving
- 5 large eggs, beaten
- 1 cup freshly grated sharp cheddar cheese
- ½ cup chopped seeded jalapeños

THIS RECIPE IS VERY VERSATILE. THE FLAVOR base is great on its own, but feel free to add chopped veggies, herbs, bacon, or ham to vary up the flavors.

Preheat the oven to 350 degrees F. Spray a mini muffin tin with nonstick spray.

In a large mixing bowl, whisk together the almond flour, coconut flour, baking powder, salt, onion powder, and garlic powder. Stir in the melted butter until blended, then stir in the eggs until blended. Fold in the cheese and jalapeños until evenly mixed into the batter. Pour the batter evenly into the prepared mini muffin tin.

Bake for 10–12 minutes, until the muffins are cooked through and golden brown. Remove from the oven and let stand for 3–4 minutes. Using a butter knife or silicone spatula, gently pop the muffins out of the tin and serve with butter.

MINI TACO CUPS

YIELD: 24 MINI TACO CUPS

PAIRED WITH WHIPPED GUAC (PAGE 111), Eight-Layer Dip (page 112), and Tortilla Chips (page 136), these mini taco cups will give you an instant party—especially if you throw in a margarita or three. For the taco seasoning, I use Eat Happy Kitchen Taco Dust Seasoning, but you can use any brand you like; just double check the label to make sure there's no added sugars or fillers. I like Tillamook brand sliced cheese.

MINI TACO CUPS

6 thick slices Colby Jack or cheddar cheese, quartered

8 ounces ground beef (I use 85% lean)

1 tablespoon Eat Happy Kitchen Taco Dust Seasoning or other no-sugar-added taco seasoning

¼ cup water

¼ cup sour cream

FOR TOPPING

Salsa

Chopped fresh chives

Chopped jalapeños

No-sugar-added hot sauce

Preheat the oven to 350 degrees F. Line a rimmed baking sheet with parchment paper.

Working in batches, arrange a single layer of quartered cheese slices on the prepared baking sheet, at least 2 inches apart. Bake for 4–5 minutes, then remove from the oven and let stand for 2–3 minutes. Using a small spatula, gently move the heated cheese squares into the cups of a mini muffin tin. Let them cool completely.

Heat a large skillet over medium-high heat. Add the ground beef and cook, breaking it up and crumbling it with a spatula, until fully cooked and browned, about 5 minutes. Remove from the heat and add the taco seasoning and water. (If you like, you can first drain off the beef fat from the pan, but I like to use it to help the taco seasoning blend into the beef.) Stir until the beef is coated in seasoning.

Portion out ½ teaspoon sour cream into each cooled cheese cup, then spoon some of the taco meat into each cheese cup. Top with salsa, chopped jalapeños, chives, and hot sauce, then serve hot.

GREEK SALAD PINWHEELS

YIELD: 12–15 PINWHEELS

6 Persian cucumbers, sliced lengthwise into thin ribbons

Salt

4 ounces feta cheese

3 tablespoons sour cream

1 teaspoon minced fresh oregano

8–10 pitted kalamata olives, finely chopped

¼ red onion, minced

8–10 cherry tomatoes, finely chopped

THESE VEGETARIAN CUCUMBER PINWHEELS are like a personal Greek salad you can eat with your fingers.

I use Persian cucumbers because they have fewer seeds. Use a vegetable peeler or the thin setting on a mandoline, or sharpen your knife and cosplay being a sushi chef. The size of the cucumber will determine the size of the final pinwheel, so try to find smaller cucumbers at the grocery store to keep the pinwheels bite-size.

On a flat work surface lined with parchment paper, lay out the cucumber slices. Lightly season the cucumbers with salt and let them "sweat" for 10 minutes, then dab them dry of any excess water.

In a small mixing bowl, use a hand mixer to beat the feta cheese and sour cream until soft, then mix in the oregano.

Using a butter knife or small spatula, spread a thin layer of the creamy feta on each cucumber slice. Sprinkle on some chopped olives, onion, and tomatoes in an even layer. Roll up each layered cucumber slice into a pinwheel and secure with a toothpick. Refrigerate for 30–60 minutes, then serve cold.

SMOKED SALMON CUCUMBER PINWHEELS

YIELD: 12–15 PINWHEELS

CUCUMBER PINWHEELS MAKE AN ELEGANT display and are especially nice for warm-weather gatherings, as they are served chilled.

I use Persian cucumbers because they have fewer seeds. Use a vegetable peeler or the thin setting on a mandoline, or sharpen your knife and cosplay being a sushi chef. The size of the cucumber will determine the size of the final pinwheel, so try to find smaller cucumbers at the grocery store to keep the pinwheels bite-size.

6 Persian cucumbers, sliced lengthwise into thin ribbons

Salt

4 ounces cream cheese, at room temperature

Juice of 1 lemon

2 tablespoons capers, drained

4 ounces smoked salmon

Dill sprigs

On a flat work surface lined with paper towels, lay out the cucumber slices. Lightly season the cucumbers with salt and let them "sweat" for 10 minutes, then dab them dry of any excess water.

In a small mixing bowl, use a hand mixer to beat the cream cheese and lemon juice until smooth.

Using a butter knife or small spatula, spread a thin layer of cream cheese on each cucumber slice. Press 3–4 capers into the cream cheese layer, down the length of the cucumber slices. Top the cream cheese with the smoked salmon, cut to fit the width of the cucumber slices. Lay a few sprigs of fresh dill in the center, then roll up each layered cucumber slice into a pinwheel. Secure with toothpicks. Refrigerate for 30–60 minutes, then serve cold.

(pictured next page)

Smoked Salmon Cucumber Pinwheels, page 145

SAVORY ZUCCHINI BALLS

YIELD: 12–16 BALLS

3 zucchini, grated on the large holes of a box grater

1½ teaspoons salt, divided

2 large eggs

½ cup almond flour or crushed pork rinds

½ teaspoon garlic powder

½ cup freshly grated Parmesan cheese

3 tablespoons cream cheese, at room temperature

HERE'S A LOVELY RECIPE FOR BRUNCH, A bridal or baby shower, or any luncheon where you'd like to replace bread with something more substantial. As a cocktail hour snack, they're terrific with marinara sauce or ranch for dipping.

Preheat the oven to 350 degrees F. Line a rimmed baking sheet with parchment paper.

Place the grated zucchini on a clean tea towel or paper towels and season with ½ teaspoon of the salt. Roll up in the towel to squeeze out as much excess water as possible.

Pour the zucchini into a large mixing bowl and add the remaining 1 teaspoon salt, the eggs, almond flour, garlic powder, grated Parmesan, and cream cheese. Mix to combine evenly into a "dough." Using a cookie scooper or a teaspoon, make 1½-inch balls and place on the lined baking sheet, at least 2 inches apart.

Bake for 24–26 minutes, until starting to turn golden brown. Remove from the oven and serve hot.

BANH MI BITES

YIELD: 20–24 BITES

ROASTED PORK BELLY

2 tablespoons olive oil

1/2 cup gluten-free soy sauce or coconut aminos

Juice of 1 lime

1 tablespoon rice vinegar

1 teaspoon lemongrass paste (usually found in a tube in the produce aisle)

1/2 teaspoon toasted sesame oil

1/2 teaspoon red pepper flakes

2–3 pounds pork belly

PICKLED VEGGIES

1/4 cup finely chopped carrot

1/4 cup finely chopped sweet onion

1/4 cup finely chopped daikon or radish

1 tablespoon finely chopped jalapeño or other chile pepper

1/2 cup rice vinegar

1/4 cup water

BANH MI IS A VIETNAMESE SANDWICH TRADItionally served on a crispy bread made from wheat and rice flour. In this simplified, low-carb, no-added-sugar version, pork belly serves as the base of the bite. Vietnamese food is fresh and perfect on its own without the need for added sugar, with the pickled veggies offsetting the richness of the pork belly.

The most time-consuming part of the recipe is marinating the pork belly and slow roasting it. Most grocery stores with a butcher department can get you a 2- or 3-pound pork belly slab from the back before they cut it into bacon.

Traditional banh mi has pâté on it for a spread, but this recipe omits it, as pâté can be tricky to find in some grocery stores in the US. If you have it, feel free to use it!

Whisk together the olive oil, soy sauce, lime juice, rice vinegar, lemongrass paste, sesame oil, and pepper flakes in a small bowl. Place the pork belly in a resealable plastic bag and pour the marinade over the pork belly. Press the air out and seal the bag.

Place the minced carrot, onion, daikon, and jalapeño in a small bowl. Pour in the vinegar and water and make sure all the veggies are submerged. Cover.

Put the bag with the pork belly and the bowl of veggies in the fridge for at least 4 hours or up to overnight.

Preheat the oven to 275 degrees F. Place the pork belly, skin side up, in a small roasting pan to capture the melted fat and juices so they don't evaporate. Roast

the pork for 2 hours. Raise the oven temperature to 450 degrees F and roast for another 20–30 minutes, until the skin is crisped and bubbly. Remove from the oven and let stand 20 minutes, then slice the pork belly into 1½-inch squares.

Drain the veggies in a fine-mesh strainer. Transfer to a paper towel–lined plate to remove excess moisture.

To assemble the banh mi bites, place the pork belly pieces on a serving platter. Whisk together the mayo, soy sauce, and sriracha until smooth, then spread atop each pork belly piece. Top each piece with a cucumber slice and another dollop of the mayo sauce. Then top with cilantro leaves and pickled veggies.

(pictured next page)

BANH MI BITES

½ cup mayonnaise

2 tablespoons gluten-free soy sauce or coconut aminos

1 tablespoon sriracha

3 Persian cucumbers, thinly sliced

2 tablespoons fresh cilantro leaves

Banh Mi Bites, page 150

BUFFALO CHICKEN STUFFED MINI PEPPERS

YIELD: 20–24 STUFFED MINI PEPPERS

BUFFALO CHICKEN DIP

1 pound boneless, skinless chicken thighs

Salt and pepper

⅓ cup Frank's RedHot sauce, plus more for serving

4 ounces cream cheese, cubed

1 tablespoon salted butter

STUFFED MINI PEPPERS

1 cup freshly grated Colby Jack or cheddar cheese

1 tablespoon chopped fresh parsley, plus more for garnish

10–12 mini sweet bell peppers (assorted colors), tops discarded, halved lengthwise, and seeded

I WOULD BE REMISS IN WRITING AN ENTIRE cookbook on low-carb happy hour and not doing something wonderful with Buffalo chicken. It's the savory, spicy, creamy taste sensation that screams football season comfort food.

The Buffalo chicken can also be made on its own for a wonderful dip, but I love the presentation in mini bell peppers.

Season the chicken thighs well with salt and pepper. *To cook in an Instant Pot:* Place the chicken thighs in an Instant Pot, pour over the hot sauce, and drop in the cream cheese cubes and butter. Cover the Instant Pot and set the vent to "Sealing." Cook for 20 minutes on the Manual setting, letting the Instant Pot pressurize and depressurize naturally. The whole cycle will take 45–55 minutes.

To cook in a slow cooker: Place the chicken thighs in the slow cooker, pour over the hot sauce, and drop in the cream cheese cubes and butter. Cover and cook on high for 3–4 hours, or until the chicken is fall-apart fork-tender.

Preheat the oven to 425 degrees F. Line a rimmed baking sheet with parchment paper.

Using culinary claws or two large forks, shred the chicken into small pieces. Transfer the shredded chicken and ½ cup of the cooking liquid to a large mixing bowl.

Add the cheese and parsley and stir with a fork until mixed well.

Arrange the pepper halves cut side up on the lined baking sheet. Scoop the chicken mixture into the pepper halves.

Bake for 12–15 minutes, or until the peppers are soft and the chicken mixture starts to turn golden brown. Remove from the oven and transfer the stuffed peppers to a serving platter. Drizzle with more hot sauce and garnish with more parsley.

BACON-WRAPPED RANCH POPPERS

YIELD: 16 POPPERS

- 1 (8-ounce) package cream cheese, at room temperature
- 1 cup freshly grated Monterey Jack, Colby Jack, or cheddar cheese
- 3/4 teaspoon dried dill
- 1/2 teaspoon onion powder
- 1/2 teaspoon garlic powder
- 1/4 teaspoon pepper
- 8 medium to large jalapeños, halved lengthwise, seeds and ribs discarded
- 16 bacon slices, halved crosswise

NOBODY HAS EVER BEEN MAD AT A BACON-wrapped jalapeño popper! Spicy, savory, and filled with melty cheese, they can be air-fried or baked in the oven for party food perfection. Note: Please use gloves while cutting and seeding the jalapeños. Trust me on this! In place of the seasonings, you can use 2 teaspoons Eat Happy Kitchen's Ranch Dust.

Preheat an air fryer or oven to 400 degrees F. If using the oven, line a rimmed baking sheet with aluminum foil.

In a medium mixing bowl, mix together the cream cheese, grated cheese, dill, onion powder, and garlic powder, using a fork to smash it until it's blended. Scoop the cheese blend into the jalapeño halves, then wrap each one with a half slice of bacon, securing the bacon with a toothpick on each end. (The bacon will shrink when it cooks and try to come off the jalapeño, so the toothpicks are necessary.)

To air-fry: Working in batches as necessary, place the jalapeño poppers in the air fryer basket. Air-fry for 13–15 minutes, until the bacon is cooked and crispy. Remove from the air fryer and let cool for 5–10 minutes, then remove the toothpicks and serve.

To bake: Place the jalapeño poppers on the lined baking sheet. Bake for 20 minutes, or until the bacon is cooked and crispy. Remove from the oven and let cool for 5–10 minutes, then remove the toothpicks and serve.

BUTTER-POACHED SHRIMP

YIELD: 6–8 APPETIZER SERVINGS

IN THE SOUTH, THERE IS BUTTER-POACHED shrimp at every gathering you go to, whether it's a cocktail party, a baby shower, a church potluck, a boozy brunch, a wake, or your third cousin's third wedding bridal party luncheon. We are taught how to butter-poach shrimp as soon as we are allowed near the stove. Serve it warm or cold. Or use it as the perfect garnish for a Meaty Mary (page 62).

- 2 pounds large shrimp, peeled and deveined, tails left on
- Salt and pepper
- Eat Happy Kitchen BBQ Dust Seasoning or other favorite BBQ rub
- 1 cup salted butter
- 4 garlic cloves, minced
- Juice of 1 lemon, plus more lemon wedges for garnish
- Chopped fresh parsley and chives, for garnish

Pat the shrimp dry. Season with salt, pepper, and BBQ seasoning.

Melt the butter in a large, flat-bottomed sauté pan over medium-high heat until bubbling. Add the garlic and cook for 1–2 minutes, until golden and fragrant. Squeeze in the lemon juice. Working in batches so as not to crowd the pan, add the shrimp and cook for 2–3 minutes per side, until cooked through and pink. Transfer to a platter.

When all the shrimp are done, pour any remaining butter in the pan over the shrimp. Sprinkle additional BBQ seasoning on the shrimp and garnish with chopped parsley and chives and wedges of lemon.

(pictured next page)

Butter-Poached Shrimp, page 159

SHERRY VINEGAR AND BUTTER SCALLOPS

YIELD: 16 SCALLOPS

16 sea scallops

Salt and pepper

6 tablespoons salted butter

1 large shallot, minced

3 tablespoons capers, drained

3 tablespoons sherry vinegar

Harissa seasoning, for garnish

HERE'S A FANCY-LOOKING DISH THAT IS SUPER simple to whip up. Make sure you pat the scallops dry before cooking them, as scallops are often injected with water to make them appear larger.

Pat the scallops dry. Place the scallops on a paper towel–lined plate and season both sides with salt and pepper.

In a large cast-iron skillet or sauté pan, melt the butter over medium-high heat until bubbling. Add the shallot and cook until soft and fragrant, 2–3 minutes. Whisk in the capers and vinegar, season with salt, and cook for 1 more minute. Add the scallops to the pan in a single layer and cook for 1–2 minutes, then flip and cook for 1 more minute, tilting the pan to spoon the butter sauce over the scallops.

Transfer the scallops to a platter, pouring any remaining butter sauce from the pan over the scallops. Garnish with a sprinkle of ground harissa and serve immediately.

CURRIED CHICKEN SALAD ON ENDIVE

YIELD: 4–5 CUPS CHICKEN SALAD (25–35 BITES)

CHICKEN SALAD IS THE BEST LUNCH FOOD there is, and I make it at least once a week. Curried chicken salad takes it to the next level, but if you get it at a restaurant or deli, it's usually loaded with sugar. This version gets us back to what we love about curry without it being full of cloying sweetness.

- 3 cups shredded or chopped cooked chicken
- 2 celery ribs, diced
- ¼ cup diced sweet onion
- 1 Granny Smith apple, peeled, cored, and finely diced
- Juice of ½ lime
- ½ cup mayonnaise
- ¼ cup plus 3 tablespoons olive oil, divided
- Salt and pepper
- 1 tablespoon curry powder
- ⅓ cup roasted salted pistachios, crushed into smaller pieces
- 3 endive heads, stems removed
- 1 tablespoon white wine vinegar
- Finely chopped fresh chives, for garnish

In a large mixing bowl, toss the chicken, celery, onion, and apple until well mixed. Squeeze the half lime over the contents of the bowl. Fold in the mayonnaise and ¼ cup of the olive oil. Season with salt and pepper. Fold in the curry powder until well mixed, then fold in the pistachios. Taste the chicken salad and, if needed, season once more with salt and pepper.

On a serving platter, lay out the endive leaves. In a small mixing bowl, whisk together the remaining 3 tablespoons olive oil and the vinegar. Season the oil and vinegar with salt and pepper. Drizzle the endive leaves with some of the dressing. Scoop bite-size dollops of the curried chicken salad onto each endive leaf. Top with chopped fresh chives and serve immediately.

CHICKEN SATAY SKEWERS WITH THAI PEANUT DIPPING SAUCE

YIELD: 6–8 SERVINGS

CHICKEN SATAY

2 pounds, boneless, skinless chicken thighs, sliced into 1-inch-wide strips

Salt and pepper

½ cup canned full-fat unsweetened coconut cream or plain full-fat Greek yogurt

2 tablespoons gluten-free soy sauce or coconut aminos

1 tablespoon red curry paste

Juice of 1 lime, plus lime wedges for garnish

1 teaspoon lemongrass paste (usually found in a tube in the produce department)

1 teaspoon grated fresh ginger

2 teaspoons curry powder

2 tablespoons coconut oil (optional)

Chopped fresh cilantro, for garnish

Chopped peanuts, for garnish

I LOVE WRITING RECIPES THAT ARE CLEAN versions of restaurant favorites, and these satay skewers rank up there with the best of them. Allow me to define "clean" for my purposes: no to gluten, grains, and sugar . . . but a big yes to flavor. And somehow these delightful chicken skewers, served fresh off the grill with homemade dipping sauce, taste better than restaurant quality.

Season the chicken thigh strips with salt and pepper.

In a large mixing bowl, whisk together the coconut cream, soy sauce, red curry paste, lime juice, lemongrass, ginger, and curry powder until smooth. Plunge the seasoned chicken thigh strips into the marinade, tossing to coat. Cover and refrigerate for 2–6 hours.

In a small saucepan, whisk together all the sauce ingredients and bring to a boil over medium heat, then reduce the heat and let simmer for 10 minutes to let the flavors meld. Stir in water 1 tablespoon at a time to thin the sauce to the desired consistency. Remove from the heat and cover to keep warm.

If using bamboo skewers, soak them in water for 10 minutes so they don't burn. Thread the chicken onto the skewers, leaving enough room at one end to handle.

To grill: Preheat a grill to 500 degrees F. Grill the chicken skewers for 5–7 minutes, flipping halfway through, until cooked through.

To sauté: Heat the coconut oil in a large cast-iron skillet or sauté pan over high heat. Working in batches as necessary, cook the chicken skewers for 5–7 minutes, flipping halfway through, until cooked through.

Garnish with cilantro and peanuts and serve immediately, with the dipping sauce and lime wedges.

THAI PEANUT DIPPING SAUCE

½ cup smooth no-sugar-added peanut butter

¼ cup canned full-fat unsweetened coconut cream or milk

¼ cup gluten-free soy sauce or coconut aminos

2 tablespoons red curry paste

Juice of 1½ limes

3 tablespoons rice wine vinegar

1 tablespoon sriracha

4–6 tablespoons water

PIGS IN A BLANKET

YIELD: 18–20 PIGGIES

- ⅔ cup almond flour or crushed pork rinds
- ½ teaspoon baking powder
- 1 teaspoon dried minced onion, plus more for garnish
- 1 teaspoon white sesame seeds, plus more for garnish
- ¼ teaspoon garlic powder
- ¼ teaspoon salt
- ⅛ teaspoon cayenne pepper
- 1½ cups freshly grated Colby Jack cheese
- 1 tablespoon cream cheese, at room temperature
- 1 large egg
- Olive oil
- 1 (14-ounce) package Lit'l Smokies cocktail links or mini sausages, or 6 hot dogs, each cut into 2-inch pieces
- 2 tablespoons melted salted butter
- 1 tablespoon Dijon mustard, plus more for serving
- Black sesame seeds, for garnish

THE QUINTESSENTIAL CLASSIC AMERICAN party food, pigs in a blanket are usually shrouded in gluten-filled puff pastry. But here we adapt my low-carb dough (which you'll also use in the Baked Brie recipe on page 108) so we get to enjoy these savory poppers without all those extra carbs. I have yet to source a super-clean cocktail weenie, so I'm using the classic Lit'l Smokies for this recipe. Maybe making clean cocktail weenies is the future of Eat Happy Kitchen?

Preheat the oven to 400 degrees F. Line a rimmed baking sheet with parchment paper.

In a large mixing bowl, whisk together the almond flour, baking powder, dried minced onion, white sesame seeds, garlic powder, salt, and cayenne. Then add the grated cheese, cream cheese, and egg and mix into a dough ball, being careful not to overmix.

Transfer the dough to a large piece of parchment paper. Dab your fingers with olive oil and press the dough ball flat to about ½-inch thickness. Cover the dough with another piece of parchment. Use a rolling pin to roll the dough between the two pieces of parchment to ¼-inch thickness, as evenly as possible. Using a pizza cutter or sharp knife, slice the dough into strips a little narrower than the width of the sausage links. Roll each sausage link in a strip of dough to wrap evenly, then use your fingers to seal off the edges. Place on the prepared baking sheet, 2 inches apart. Bake for 10–12

minutes, or until the "blanket" shells are golden brown. Remove from the oven.

While the piggies cook, whisk together the melted butter and mustard in a small mixing bowl. When the piggies come out of the oven, brush the tops with the butter-mustard mixture. Garnish each piggie with black and white sesame seeds and dried minced onion. Serve with Dijon mustard.

AVO-BACON BITES

YIELD: 16–18 BITES

I LIKE TO MAKE THESE AS A LOW-CARB SNACK or appetizer. Who wouldn't love creamy avocado rolled in freshly made bacon bits? Amp up the heat with extra cayenne if you're feeling spicy.

- 2 avocados, pitted, peeled, and sliced
- 4 ounces cream cheese, at room temperature
- 1 tablespoon minced sweet onion
- Salt and pepper
- 1/8 teaspoon cayenne pepper
- 1 pound bacon, cooked until crispy and crumbled into bits

In a medium mixing bowl, use a fork to mash the avocado, cream cheese, and minced onion into a chunky guacamole. Season with salt, pepper, and the cayenne, and stir once more. Cover and place in the fridge to set up for 30 minutes.

Remove the avocado mixture from the fridge. Place the bacon bits on a plate. To make each bite, use a cookie scooper or teaspoon to scoop out a 1-inch dollop of the avocado mixture and roll it gently in the bacon bits. Place on a platter and serve immediately, or refrigerate for another 30 minutes before serving for firmer bites.

Dill Pickle Tots, page 174

DILL PICKLE TOTS

YIELD: 16–18 TOTS

- 1 (16-ounce) bag cauliflower rice, or 1 head cauliflower grated on a box grater
- 1 red or green jalapeño, seeded and finely chopped
- 1 cup freshly grated sharp cheddar cheese
- ¼ cup finely chopped dill pickle
- 2 tablespoons dill pickle juice
- 1 tablespoon Eat Happy Kitchen Ranch Dust or other natural ranch seasoning
- 1 large egg, beaten

IT'S DILL PICKLE EVERYTHING THESE DAYS! Once I saw dill pickle Tater Tots on a bar menu, but their version was just regular potato tots covered in relish. Boring. My recipe incorporates the flavor into the tot itself. Of course, this isn't really a potato tot, but a veggie croquette with steamed cauliflower at the heart of it. For extra pickle bliss, serve with Dill Pickle Ranch Dip (page 96).

Preheat the oven to 350 degrees F. Line a rimmed baking sheet with parchment paper.

Snip off one corner of the cauliflower rice bag with scissors and microwave the bag for 4 minutes. (Or, if using grated fresh cauliflower, pour the rice into a microwave-safe bowl, fill with 2 inches of water, cover with plastic wrap, and microwave for 4 minutes). Drain the cauliflower rice in a fine-mesh strainer.

Transfer the cauliflower rice to a clean tea towel and roll it up to soak up any excess water. Let the towel sit for 10 minutes. Press out the water into the towel one more time, then pour the cauliflower into a mixing bowl. Add the jalapeño, cheddar, and pickle and toss to combine. Stir in the pickle juice and ranch seasoning. Fold in the egg and combine evenly.

Using your hands, form the mixture into tot shapes and place on the prepared baking sheet, about 1 inch apart. Bake for 20–25 minutes, until golden brown. Remove from the oven and let stand for 3–5 minutes before serving.

BACON BEEF MINI SMASH SLIDERS

YIELD: 35 SLIDERS

SLIDERS ARE A GREAT LOW-CARB PARTY FOOD option. Here we combine components to save us from building a messy slider that would need a bun to hold it all together: Mustard goes in with the onions, bacon goes into the burger blend.

For the tomatoes, you want smaller than a regular vine-ripened tomato, but larger than a cherry or grape tomato so that the width of the slice fits perfectly on your slider. I've found "cocktail" tomatoes at my local store, but they may be called something different at yours.

- 2 tablespoons olive oil
- 1 large onion, thinly sliced
- ½ teaspoon salt, plus more for seasoning
- ¼ teaspoon garlic powder
- ¼ teaspoon onion powder
- 2 tablespoons white wine vinegar
- 1 tablespoon stone-ground mustard
- 1 pound ground beef (85% lean)
- 4 thick-cut bacon slices, cut into small cubes
- 1 tablespoon yellow mustard
- 1 tablespoon gluten-free soy sauce or coconut aminos
- Pepper
- Sliced cheese of choice, cut into 1½-inch squares
- 3–4 small tomatoes, thinly sliced
- Dill pickle slices

Heat the olive oil in a large, flat-bottomed sauté pan over medium-high heat until shimmering. Add the onion and cook, tossing frequently, until soft and starting to sear, 4–5 minutes. Stir in the salt, garlic powder, onion powder, and vinegar. Turn the heat down to medium-low, cover the pan, and let the onion cook for 30–45 minutes, until soft and caramelized, stirring every 15 minutes. Remove from the heat and stir in the stone-ground mustard until blended in. Transfer the caramelized onion to a plate. Reserve the pan for the burgers.

In a large mixing bowl, combine the ground beef, bacon, yellow mustard, and soy sauce and mix well. Roll the mixture into 1-inch balls. Heat the reserved pan over medium-high heat. Working in batches as necessary, place a few meatballs a few inches apart in the

continued on next page

continued from previous page

hot pan. Using a spatula, smash down the balls into mini patties. Season the patties with salt and pepper. Cook for 2–3 minutes, then flip the patties and cook for 2–3 more minutes. Using a spoon, scoop some caramelized onion on top of each burger, then lay a cheese square on top. Cover and let the cheese melt for 1–2 minutes, then transfer the burgers to a serving platter.

To assemble the sliders, top each burger with a tomato slice and a pickle slice, holding everything together with a toothpick.

RAFIK'S LAMB LOLLIES WITH HOMEMADE TZATZIKI

YIELD: 4–6 SERVINGS AND 2½ CUPS TZATZIKI

LAMB LOLLIES

2–3 pounds French-cut lamb chops

Salt and pepper

¼ cup balsamic vinegar

¼ cup gluten-free soy sauce or coconut aminos

¼ cup olive oil

1 teaspoon dried oregano

1 teaspoon minced garlic

HOMEMADE TZATZIKI

5 Persian cucumbers or 1 large English cucumber, peeled and roughly chopped

2 teaspoons salt, plus more for cucumbers

1 tablespoon chopped fresh dill

1 garlic clove, chopped

2 tablespoons lemon juice

2 cups plain full-fat Greek yogurt

Pepper

IMAGINE, IF YOU WILL . . . A SPHINX, A PHARAOH, and a hellion, all embodied within one droll-faced Lebanese-Egyptian man. Then imagine this man waving freshly grilled lamb lollies and Sangiovese in your face. You would pay attention.

I strategically surround myself with people who love to cook. My friend Rafik and his wife, Michelle, make fantastic food, so I know that if I'm going to their house, I'm gonna be eating like a rock star. It's always going to be a good night when Rafik's lamb lollies make an appearance.

I convinced Rafik to let me adapt his recipe for his famous lamb lollies. I use balsamic vinegar in place of his beloved Sangiovese. Plus you can use regular cut lamb chops instead of French cut, but you still have to eat them fresh off the grill with your bare hands.

Season the lamb chops well with salt and pepper. In a small mixing bowl, whisk together the balsamic vinegar, soy sauce, olive oil, oregano, and garlic. Pour into a resealable plastic bag. Place the lamb chops in the bag, press out the air, and seal it, then swish the marinade all over the lamb chops until completely coated. Refrigerate for at least 2 hours or up to overnight.

Meanwhile, on a flat work surface lined with paper towels, lay out the cucumber pieces. Lightly season the cucumbers with salt and let them "sweat" for 10 minutes, then dab them dry of any excess water. In a food

processor or high-speed blender, combine the cucumber pieces, dill, garlic, lemon juice, salt, and pepper. Pulse until blended but still chunky, then transfer the contents to a small bowl. Whisk in the Greek yogurt. Cover and refrigerate until ready to serve.

Preheat the grill to 500–550 degrees F. Remove the lamb chops from the fridge 30 minutes before cooking. Grill the lamb chops for 1–2 minutes per side, then serve with the tzatziki.

Rafik's Lamb Lollies, page 178

SPINACH DIP LOW-CARB CRUST CHRISTMAS TREE

YIELD: 6–8 SERVINGS

CRUST

Avocado, coconut, or olive oil nonstick spray

1½ cups freshly grated Colby Jack, mozzarella, or cheddar cheese

1¼ cups almond flour or crushed pork rinds

2 ounces cream cheese, at room temperature

2 large eggs, beaten

½ teaspoon garlic powder

½ teaspoon onion powder

SPINACH DIP

8 ounces frozen chopped spinach, thawed and pressed dry with paper towels

4 ounces cream cheese

¾ cup grated Gruyère cheese

4 large egg yolks

¼ teaspoon salt

¼ teaspoon garlic powder

¼ teaspoon onion powder

TO SERVE

Chopped cherry tomatoes or red bell peppers

Dill Pickle Ranch Dip (page 96; optional)

TREE-SHAPED ANYTHING ON CHRISTMAS IS deliciously festive. The carb version uses puff pastry, but we are bringing the low-carb spin in-house to make an adorable tree. Serve with Eggnog (page 48) and good cheer.

Preheat the oven to 350 degrees F. Line a rimmed baking sheet with parchment paper. With a pencil, draw the outline of a Christmas tree on the parchment, taking up most of the space on the baking sheet. Spray with nonstick spray.

In a mixing bowl, combine all the crust ingredients well into a dough ball. Tip the dough ball out onto the lined baking sheet. Press the dough into the tree outline until ½ inch thick. Pierce with a fork several times. Bake for 10 minutes, or until starting to turn golden brown. Remove the crust from the oven.

Meanwhile, in a large mixing bowl, using a hand mixer, mix together all the spinach dip filling ingredients until blended. Press the spinach dip onto the crust, leaving about ¼ inch crust exposed all around the edges. Return the baking sheet to the oven and bake for 13–15 minutes, until the spinach dip is cooked and the edges of the crust are turning brown.

Remove from the oven and trim the tree with chopped cherry tomatoes and/or red bell peppers. Using a pizza slicer, cut the servings to look like branches of the tree. Serve with ranch dip on the side, if you like.

Mini Vanilla Fruit Tarts, page 192

SWEET BITES

My philosophy is always to include a few sweet recipes in my books because life is meant to be celebrated. This is a party book, after all! With these yummy sweet bite recipes, you can serve your guests homemade, grain-free sweets made with as little sugar as possible.

I use only natural sweeteners. If you like sugar substitutes and/or artificial sweeteners, have at it, but I don't work with those ingredients, so you will have to do your own research and experimentation to substitute them.

If these recipes are at all triggering, please rip these final pages out of the book and burn them. Does that seem extreme? It is! You can also just not make these recipes. But I've found that 100 percent of people who quit sugar eat it again at some point in their lives. So why not offer up a high-quality sweet treat that is made with love?

MINI ESPRESSO CHEESECAKE BOMBS

YIELD: 24 BITES

MUD CRUST

- Avocado or coconut oil nonstick spray
- 2/3 cup almond flour
- 1/3 cup unsweetened cocoa powder
- 1/3 cup coconut sugar
- 1/2 cup salted butter, melted

FILLING

- 2 (8-ounce) packages cream cheese, at room temperature
- 1/2 cup sour cream
- 1/4 cup unsweetened cocoa powder
- 1/4 cup coconut sugar
- 1/2 cup espresso or strong brewed coffee, cooled
- 1 teaspoon no-sugar-added vanilla extract
- Dark (85% cacao) chocolate, shaved, for garnish

THIS IS THE FIFTH OR SIXTH CHEESECAKE recipe that I've published. Honestly, I've lost count. I am officially obsessed with cheesecake. This time we're adding coffee and a "mud" crust on the bottom. When you eat one or two of these, you will feel so satisfied about everything in your life (or at least that you made and ate these cheesecake bombs).

Preheat the oven to 350 degrees F. Spray a mini muffin tin with nonstick spray.

In a large mixing bowl, whisk together the almond flour, cocoa powder, and coconut sugar. Pour in the melted butter and stir to combine well. Press the dough into the cups of the prepared mini muffin tin, making sure to bring the dough up the sides of the muffin cups. Bake for 10–12 minutes, or until the crust starts to become fragrant. Remove from the oven and let cool for 10–15 minutes, then use the back of a spoon to press the crusts down again before letting cool completely.

In a large mixing bowl, using a hand mixer, combine the cream cheese, sour cream, cocoa powder, espresso, and vanilla until smooth. Using a cookie scooper or tablespoon, scoop the filling into the cooled crusts in the mini muffin tin. Refrigerate for at least 2–4 hours, until fully chilled.

To serve, use a butter knife to cut around the edges of the crust and then pop out the mini cheesecake bombs. Arrange on a serving platter and garnish with shaved dark chocolate.

LEMON BARS

YIELD: 16 (2-INCH) BARS

WHILE I OFTEN LIKE TO USE A NATURAL sweetener like coconut sugar or coconut nectar when making my sweet treats, this recipe will look the best if you use regular white sugar to maintain a bright, sunny lemon color.

CRUST

- Avocado or coconut oil nonstick spray
- 1½ cups almond flour
- 2 tablespoons sugar
- ½ cup salted butter, melted
- 1 teaspoon no-sugar-added vanilla extract

FILLING

- ½ cup sugar
- 1 tablespoon grated lemon zest, plus ½ cup lemon juice (from 2–3 lemons)
- 3 tablespoons arrowroot powder
- ½ teaspoon baking powder
- 3 large eggs
- Powdered sugar, for dusting (optional)

Preheat the oven to 350 degrees F with a rack in the center of the oven. Spray an 8 x 8-inch baking pan with nonstick spray.

In a medium mixing bowl, combine the almond flour, sugar, melted butter, and vanilla. Form into a dough ball. Press the dough ball evenly into the prepared pan, pressing the edges slightly up the sides of the pan. Bake for 12–14 minutes, or until the crust is starting to turn golden brown and become fragrant. Remove from the oven and let cool for 5 minutes. Leave the oven on.

While the crust is baking, whisk together the sugar, lemon zest and juice, arrowroot, baking powder, and eggs until smooth. Pour the filling over the slightly cooled crust.

Bake for 20–22 minutes, until the center jiggles slightly but is set. Remove from the oven and let cool completely, then refrigerate for 1–2 hours before cutting into 16 squares. Dust the bars with powdered sugar before serving, if desired.

FUDGY BROWNIE BITES
WITH DARK CHOCOLATE GLAZE

YIELD: 20–22 BITES

Avocado or coconut oil nonstick spray

1/2 cup coconut flour

1/2 cup unsweetened cocoa powder

1 teaspoon baking powder

1/2 teaspoon salt

1/2 cup coconut sugar or regular white sugar

2 large eggs

1 teaspoon no-sugar-added vanilla extract

1/2 cup whole milk

1/4 cup melted coconut oil

Maldon sea salt flakes, for garnish

DARK CHOCOLATE GLAZE

2 ounces dark (85% cacao) chocolate

1 tablespoon melted coconut oil

1 teaspoon honey or coconut nectar (optional)

THESE BITES LIVE SOMEWHERE BETWEEN A brownie and a cake pop because of the nature of baking with grain-free ingredients. They're delicious, low in sugar, and the perfect treat bite when the chocolate cravings hit at the party.

Preheat the oven to 350 degrees F. Spray a mini muffin tin with nonstick spray.

Sift the coconut flour and cocoa powder into a medium mixing bowl, then whisk in the baking powder, salt, and sugar.

In a large mixing bowl, whisk together the eggs, vanilla, and milk until smooth. Whisk the dry ingredients into the wet ingredients, in three stages, until blended. Mix in the melted coconut oil until smooth.

Evenly scoop heaping teaspoons of batter into the prepared mini muffin tin. Bake for 15–18 minutes, or until a toothpick inserted into one of the brownie bites comes out clean. Remove from the oven and let cool for 15–20 minutes.

In a microwave-safe bowl, whisk together all the glaze ingredients. Microwave in 30-second bursts, stirring after each, until melted and smooth. (Alternatively, you can melt the glaze in a double boiler on the stovetop.)

Remove the cooled brownie bites to a serving platter and pour the glaze over them. Top each bite with a few sprinkles of Maldon sea salt flakes before serving.

MINI VANILLA FRUIT TARTS

YIELD: 24 MINI TARTS

CRUST

- Avocado or coconut oil nonstick spray
- 1 cup almond flour
- 1 tablespoon coconut flour
- ¼ teaspoon salt
- 2 tablespoons sugar
- 1 teaspoon grated lemon zest
- 5 tablespoons unsalted butter, cubed
- 1 teaspoon no-sugar-added vanilla extract

FRUIT TART CUSTARD FILLING

- 5 large egg yolks
- ¼ cup sugar
- 1 cup whole milk
- 1 cup heavy cream
- 2 teaspoons no-sugar-added vanilla extract or vanilla bean paste
- Mixed berries (such as raspberries, blackberries, sliced strawberries, or blueberries)
- Fresh mint leaves, for garnish (optional)
- Powdered sugar, for garnish (optional)

AS WITH MY LEMON BARS (PAGE 189), I PREFER to use regular white sugar in the filling for these tarts so that the vanilla custard keeps a pale vanilla color. You are welcome to use honey or coconut sugar, but if the sweetener is too dark, you will end up with a brown custard.

If you can find no-sugar-added vanilla paste in the baking section of your grocery store, then I suggest trying that in the custard. And as always, if you're feeling luxurious, use a whole vanilla bean: Simmer it in the custard for 10 minutes, then slice it open and scrape out those delicious tiny flavor bumps into the custard. Discard the spent pod while continuing to cook the custard.

Preheat the oven to 350 degrees F. Spray a mini muffin tin with nonstick spray.

In a medium mixing bowl, whisk together the almond flour, coconut flour, and salt. In a small bowl, with clean hands, combine the sugar and lemon zest, massaging to release the lemon oil from the zest into the sugar. Add the lemon sugar to the large bowl with the dry ingredients, whisking to combine. Add the butter cubes and vanilla and use a fork or pastry cutter to cut the butter into the dry ingredients until you form a dough.

Press the dough into the cups of the prepared mini muffin tin, making sure to bring the dough up the sides of the muffin cups; the crust should be about ¼ inch thick. Score the edges of each cup, if desired, for a more "fancy" finished edge. Bake for 8–10 minutes, until the tart shells are fragrant and turning golden brown. Remove from the oven and let cool for 5–10 minutes, but not completely.

Using a butter knife or small spatula, carefully remove the tart shells from the pan.

In a large mixing bowl, whisk together the egg yolks and sugar until they are creamy and blended. In a large saucepan, combine the milk, cream, and vanilla and bring to a low boil, stirring frequently with a wooden spoon and being careful not to let the milk scald. Remove from the heat.

Very slowly whisk a little of the hot milk mixture into the egg mixture, adding more and more hot milk to temper the eggs (that means getting them to the same temperature as the milk without letting them scramble). Pour the tempered egg mixture back into the pan. Bring to a light boil over medium heat and cook for 10–12 minutes, until the mixture starts to thicken. To test thickness, when you lift the wooden spoon up, the mixture should coat the spoon, and when you swipe your finger across it, it will leave a line. Pour the custard into a glass bowl and cover with a piece of plastic wrap to keep a skin from forming. Refrigerate for at least 2–4 hours.

Scoop a dollop of custard into each tart shell. Then place a few berries on top. Garnish with a mint leaf, if desired, and sift a bit of powdered sugar on top, then place them on your prettiest platter for serving or refrigerate until ready to serve.

(pictured on page 184)

Mini Espresso Cheesecake Bombs, page 186

ACKNOWLEDGMENTS

THANK YOU to Claire Schulz, Leah Wilson, Ariel Jewett, Sarah Avinger, Isabelle Rubio, Monica Lowry, Lindsay Marshall, Alicia Kania, Susan Welte, Adrienne Lang, and Glenn Yeffeth, Rachel Phares, Karen Wise, Ashley Casteel, Lisa Story, and the whole team at BenBella Books. You have such a gift at taking my raw material and crafting it into stellar books.

Thank you to Allison Sobczak for suggesting the concept for this book on a livestream, and then I couldn't get it out of my head ever since. One day we'll get to eat apps together in person until our hearts and stomachs explode.

Thank you to my agent, Amy Collins, for shepherding yet another cookbook into the world and continually knowing the right words to say to get me out of literary retirement.

Thank you to Vinnie Tortorich, my podcast brother and fitness sherpa. I still have your bottle of scotch waiting for you fourteen years later.

Thank you to Paul Ramos, Amy Ramos, Lesa Tucker, Eric Hollis, and Craig Wood for being my hand models.

Thank you to Tricia Clark for styling photos in this book so beautifully and for teaching me to "mise it out." You make my work so much better, and I hope one day we get to do a cooking show together.

Thank you to Kelli Beaton, my sister in arms, my travel companion, and the friend who is not only guaranteed to have the pretty barware that I can photograph cocktails in, but will be there to drink them with me after the cameras are down for the night.

Thank you to Rafik and Michelle Tadros for letting me adapt lamb lollies for the book. Your support and love of Eat Happy Kitchen means the world to me.

Thank you to Nancy Carithers and Haven Long, my food and bev mentors, teachers, and truly my family. What an honor and blessing it was to meet Haven that fateful day at St. Andrew's concert choir practice, and Nancy not long after I moved in (and you put an Oh Be Joyful in my hand).

Thank you to Matt Kelley and Todd Hauerland, my Eat Happy Kitchen cofounders and dearest friends. Who knew that all those cocktails we mixed together over the years would prepare us for the CPG business?

To my kitchen right hand, Torri Anders, without whom none of these books would exist. No one gets me more excited to create in the kitchen than you do. We always seem to find a way to get it all done, and that's 99 percent due to you. Thank you.

And finally, thank you to my husband, Loren, whose support is unwavering and whose Moscow mule is second to none; to my daughter, Lucy, whose independence and devotion to martini-stirring excellence makes me beam with pride; and to our late, beloved Izzy, the original party dawg who couldn't resist stealing the rosé right out of your glass when you weren't looking.

AGAVE AZUL
EXTRACCIÓN ÚNICA

INDEX

Page numbers in italics refer to photographs

T

V

W

Y

Z

ABOUT THE AUTHOR

Photo Credit: Joanna DeGeneres

ANNA VOCINO is a talented culinary personality and tastemaker who brings to the table a wealth of experience as a bestselling author, actor (catch her as Mrs. Potato Head in *Toy Story 5*), stand-up comedian, and founder of Eat Happy Kitchen, a natural food company making organically sourced, gluten-free, grain-free, and filler-free foods with no sugar added. Anna has created hundreds of recipes that have appeared in her bestselling cookbooks, *Eat Happy* and *Eat Happy Too*, and on her website, AnnaVocino.com, Substack, and her popular Instagram account. As a respected voice within the clean-eating community, Anna can deftly transform almost any recipe into a healthy version of the dish without sacrificing taste. Anna's recipes and expertise on everything from spices to kitchen appliances have been featured in *Women's Health*, *Parade*, *Consumer Reports*, *Real Simple*, *SELF Magazine*, Allrecipes, and other consumer media outlets.